Tax List
of
Berks County
Pennsylvania
1767

Reprinted from
Pennsylvania Archives

HERITAGE BOOKS
2006

HERITAGE BOOKS

AN IMPRINT OF HERITAGE BOOKS, INC.

Books, CDs, and more—Worldwide

For our listing of thousands of titles see our website
at
www.HeritageBooks.com

Published 2006 by
HERITAGE BOOKS, INC.
Publishing Division
65 East Main Street
Westminster, Maryland 21157-5026

Other books by the Pennsylvania Archives:
CD: Pennsylvania Archives: Second Series, Volume 3

International Standard Book Number: 978-1-58549-129-2

CONTENTS

INTRODUCTION

The following persons were taxed:
(1) Householders or landholders including land owners and tenants – no distinction was made between the two.
(2) Inmates, meaning residents in the household of another (not a renter) who worked for the landowner.
(3) Freemen, who were single men over the age of 21. They appear at the end of the listing of the township and were always assessed the same amount.
(4) Non-residents, unseated landowners (unoccupied land).

This listing was taken exactly as written in the published Third Series of Pennsylvania Archives. The spelling of names has not been changed.

Abbreviations have the following meanings.

b. smith or b'smith – blacksmith
f. – ferry, forge or furnace
f.m. – fulling mill
g.m. – grist mill
h.m. – hemp mill
m. – miller
m.h. – malt house
o.m. – oil mill

p.m. – paper mill
s. – still
s.f. – steel forge
s.m. – saw mill
s.q. – stone quarry
t.k. – tavern keeper
w.s.q. – whetstone quarry
wid'o – widow

F. Edward Wright
Westminster, Maryland

v

Proprietary Return

County of Berks - 1767

- - -

Reading Town

	Houses	Lots	Horses	Cattle	Sheep	Tax
George Albert, taverner	1	1	---	---	---	6
Peter Alstadt, sadler	1	1/2	---	1	---	4
Michael Algeier, labourer	---	---	---	---	---	1
Jacob Alder, mason	1	1	---	---	---	1
Frederick Alder	1	1	---	---	---	1
Ludwig Beyerly, fisherman	1	1	---	---	---	3
Adam Boeckley, taylor	1	1	---	---	---	1
Martin Beyer, labourer	1	1	4	1	---	6
Jacob Balde, shoemaker	1	1	---	---	---	1
Jonas Baum, butcher	1	1	1	1	---	3
Conrad Bab, tinman	1	1/2	---	1	---	2
Jacob Buchard, mason	2	1	---	1	---	2
John Baker	1	1	---	2	---	1
John Braun, shoemaker	1	1	2	1	---	3
Joseph Berrett, carpenter	1	1	---	1	---	2
Michael Block	1	1	---	1	---	1
Henry Bingeman, farmer	1	---	4	3	4	18
George Born	1	1	---	1	---	1
Mathias Buchman, mason	1	1 1/2	---	1	---	3
Stophel Boyer	1	1	---	---	---	4
John Bechtold	1	1	---	---	---	1
Jacob Burchardt, weaver	1	1	---	1	---	1
Anthony Blum, labourer	1	1	---	1	---	1
Michael Brecht, sadler	1	1	3	2	1	20
Peter Brecht, taverner	2	2	1	1	---	5
Abraham Bleistein	1	1	---	---	---	2
Fredrick Berlet, carpenter	1	1	---	1	---	1
Conrad Braun	1	1	---	1	---	2
Joseph Brendlinger	1	1	---	1	---	1
Paul Barlet, carpenter	1	1	---	1	---	1
George Bernhard, skinner	1	1	---	1	---	3
Peter Baum, turner	2	2	3	2	---	8
Edward Biddle, Esq'r,, att'y at law	1	1	---	---	---	12
Christian Broatsman	---	---	---	---	---	1
John Collier, taylor	1	1/2	1	1	---	3
William Chandlee, cutler	1	1	---	1	---	2
Jacob Commerer, taverner	1	1	1	1	---	3
Mathias Commerer, shoemaker	1	1	---	1	---	1
Henry Christ, Esq'r, justice pea.	2	2 1/2	1	1	---	12
Peter Diem, cordwainer	1	1	---	1	---	3
Yost Dietz	---	---	---	---	---	1
Garret Dewees, labourer	1	1	---	---	---	2
Ludwig Deivil	1	1	---	1	---	2
Thomas Diem	1	1	---	---	---	1
Nicholas Dick, mason	1	1/2	---	1	---	1
Adam Drinckhouse, wagoner	1	2	6	1	---	3
Henry Degenhard, tinman	1	1	1	1	---	4
Sarah Drury	---	---	---	---	---	14
James Diemer, Esq'r, Just. peace	1	1 1/2	1	1	---	9

1

	Houses	Lots	Horses	Cattle	Sheep	Tax
George Eisenbeis, mason	1	1	--	1	--	1
Adam Egee	1	1	--	1	--	1
William Ermel, mason	1	3	1	2	--	5
Martin Egee	1	1	--	--	--	1
William Erman, taylor	1	1	--	--	--	1
Ludwig Embler, blue dyer	2	1	1	1	--	3
Anthony Fricker, shopkeeper	1	1	1	1	--	8
Michael Figthorn	2	2	--	1	--	3
Nicholas Felix	--	--	--	--	--	1
Lorentz Fix, cooper	1	1/2	--	1	--	1
Feather Feather, taverner	1	1	3	2	--	7
Christian Fisher, cordw'r	1	1	--	--	--	2
Durst. Fister, cordwainer	1	1	1	1	--	2
David Fox, cooper	1	1	--	1	--	4
Fulweiler John	1	1	1	1	--	3
Nicholas Felix, shoemaker	--	--	--	1	--	1
Andreas Figthorn	1	1	--	1	--	1
Isaac Fillickey, mason	--	--	--	--	--	1
John Fry, potter	1	1	1	1	--	2
Nicholas Godschall, locksmith	1	1	1	--	--	1
Francis Gibson, labourer	1	1	--	1	--	1
Christop'r Gross, labourer	1	1	--	1	--	2
Michael Grous, baker	1	1	--	--	--	3
George Geisler, joiner	1	1/2	--	--	--	1
Jacob Grove, hatter	1	1	--	--	--	3
John Gross, bookbinder	1	1	--	--	--	3
Frederick Gordy, landlord	1	1	--	--	--	3
Bastian Grouser, carpenter	1	1	--	1	--	2
Henry Gosler, baker	1	1 1/2	--	1	--	4
William Graff, gunsmith	1	1	--	1	--	6
John Hartley, joiner	--	--	--	--	--	1
Wolfgang Haga, gunsmith	2	2	--	--	--	5
Leonard Hoch, yoeman	1	1	--	1	--	4
John Hardman, taylor	1	1/2	--	1	--	2
Peter Holtzeder, cooper	1	1	--	1	--	4
Samuel Huth, hatter	1	1	--	--	--	1
Geo. Huber, weaver	--	--	--	--	--	2
Croft Heiner, baker	1	2	1	1	--	9
John Harff, labourer	1	1	--	1	--	1
Henry Holler, taylor	1	2 1/2	1	1	--	6
Michael Haag	1	1	--	--	--	1
Thomas Hughes, carpenter	1	1	--	1	--	2
Jacob Hoffman, yeoman	1	1/2	1	1	--	2
Peter Haas, mason	1	1	--	1	--	1
Henry Hahn, blacksmith	1	1	1	1	--	8
John Hartman, miller	1	1	--	1	--	5
John Jerriger	1	1	1	--	--	4
George Jerger, gent.	1	1	--	1	--	6
Myer Josephson, shopkeeper	1	1	2	1	--	10
John Jacob	1	1	--	--	--	1
John Judy, wagoner	1	1	4	1	--	2
Sam'l Jackson, hatter	1	1	1	1	--	4
Jacob Jager, taverner	2	1 1/2	2	2	--	6
Nich's Kauffeld, cooper	--	--	--	--	--	1
Alex'r Klinger, taverner	2	2	--	1	--	5

Reading Town	Houses	Lots	Horses	Cattle	Sheep	Tax
Philip Klinger, taverner	2	2	--	1	--	6
Michael Koch	1	1	--	1	--	1
William Koch	1	1	--	1	--	1
Frederick Kast	1	1/2	1	1	--	2
Jacob Kraul, taverner	1	2	1	1	--	6
Valentine Kerber, taverner	1	1 1/2	1	1	--	8
Abram Kerber	1	1	--	1	--	2
Dan'l Adam Kurr	1	1	--	--	--	1
Conrad Kuch, potter	1	1	--	--	--	1
Michael Klein, shoemaker	1	1	1	1	--	1
Nicholas Keim, shopkeeper	2	4	2	1	--	18
Henry Keller, turner	1	1	--	1		12
John Kurtz	1	1	1	1	--	2
Martin Kraft	1	1	--	1	--	2
John Koehler	--	--	--	--	--	1
Martin Kost	1	1	--	1	--	5
Conrad Kraft	1	1/2	--	--	--	2
Jacob Keyser	1	1	4	2	--	10
Henry Krimler, potter	1	1	--	--	--	2
Isaac Levan, farmer	2	3	1	1	--	14
George Leibrand, brickmaker	--	--	--	--	--	2
Isaac Lott	--	--	--	--	--	1
Jacob Leibrook, baker	1	1	--	1	--	2
Benj'a Leimbach, taylor	--	--	--	1	--	1
Isaac Levan, Jr., tanner	1	8	2	2	--	14
Benjamin Lightfoot, storekeeper	1	2	1	1	--	22
Lorentz Leepley	1	1	--	--	--	1
Nicholas Madery, mason	1	1	--	1	--	2
Frederick Meyerly, tobaconist	1	1/2	1	1	--	2
Baltzer Meyerly, mason	1	1	--	1	--	3
John Merge, labourer	1	1	--	--	--	1
William Miller, pump maker	1	2	--	1	--	4
Christian Maurer, taverner	--	2	--	1	--	7
Christian Merckel, blacksmith	1	2	1	1	--	6
Conrad Meyer	1	1	--	--	--	3
Philip Meath, gent.	1	1	--	1	--	5
Nicholas Morris, yeoman	1	1	1	1	--	2
Geo. Meyer	1	1	--	1	--	2
Conrad Meyerly	1	1	--	--	--	2
George Menkis	1	1	--	1	--	1
Geo. Ernst Maurer	1	1	--	--	--	--
Peter Miller	1	1	--	1	--	2
Geo. Marx, mason	1	1	--	1	--	1
Henry Meyer	1	1	--	1	--	1
Dewald Miller	--	--	--	--	--	1
Wm. Marx, mason	1	1	--	--	--	1
Mathias Meyer	1	1	--	2	--	2
Isaac Morris, joiner	1	1	--	--	--	2
Mich'l Neidley, joiner	--	--	--	--	--	1
Philip Naugle	1	1	--	1	--	1
Jacob Neithack, shoem'k'r	1	1	--	--	--	3
Christ'r Neidley, alehokeeper	1	1/2	1	1	--	3
Geo. Naugle, cryer court	1	1	1	--	--	2
John Patton, Esq'r, just. pea	2	1 1/2	1	2	--	15
Benj'a Pearson, carpenter	1	1	--	1	--	5

3

Reading Town	Houses	Lots	Horses	Cattle	Sheep	Tax
Elijah Pearson, carpenter	1	1	--	1	--	2
Benj'a Parks, joiner	1	1	--	1	--	2
John Philippe	1	1	--	1	--	2
John Price, Esq'r, att'y at law	1	3/4	--	--	--	7
Leonard Reeser, labourer	1	1	--	--	--	1
Henry Rule, labourer	1	1	--	1	--	1
Mich'l Rush Sen'r, carpenter	1	1	--	1	--	1
Mich'l Rush, Jun'r, carpenter	1	1	--	1	--	2
David Rowland	--	--	--	--	--	1
Peter Rapp, butcher	1	1	1	1	--	6
Michael Rightmoyer, labourer	--	1	--	--	--	1
Henry Rightmoyer, wheelwright	1	1/2	--	1	--	3
John Rightmoyer, sadler	1	1	--	1	--	2
James Read, Esq'r, prot. just. pe.	1	3	1	--	--	15
William Reeser, gent.	1	1	1	1	--	9
Earhard Rose, taverner	1	1	--	1	--	5
Philip Ruppert	1	1	--	1	--	1
Leonard Ruppert, aleho. keeper	1	1/2	1	1	--	3
William Russell, taylor	1	1/2	--	--	--	1
David Rein, glazier	1	1	--	1	--	4
Jacob Rabbold, brickmaker	3	4	2	1	2	6
Josiah Reese, shoemaker	1	1	--	1	--	1
Nicho's Seitzinger, innkeeper	2	2	1	1	--	12
Jacob Seider, labourer	1	1	2	1	--	3
Michael Spatz	1	1	--	--	--	1
Philip Smith, joiner	2	2	--	1	--	5
Mich'l Schectelle	1	1	--	1	--	1
Fred'k Steef, shoemaker	1	1/2	--	--	--	1
Geo. Schryer, gun smith	1	--	--	--	--	1
Conrad Scheffer	1	1	--	--	--	2
Henry Senger, skinner	1	1	--	1	--	6
James Sands, joiner	1	1	--	1	--	4
Adam Sleagle, taylor	1	1	1	1	--	7
Jacob Shoemaker, taverner	1	2	1	1	--	7
Andrew Shenck, sheelr't	1	1	--	1	--	4
Sam'l Schultz, b'smith	1	1	--	1	--	2
Fred'k Seiber	1	1	--	--	--	1
Gabriel Shop, sadler	1	1	--	1	--	4
Peter Schilif	--	--	--	--	--	1
Mich'l Stump, painter	--	--	--	--	--	1
Henry Scheirer, stocking weaver	--	--	--	--	--	1
Nicholas Slichter, mason	1	1	--	1	--	2
Henry Schumaker, mason	1	1	--	1	--	2
James Scull, surveyor	1	2 1/2	2	1	--	5
Joseph Schreck	1	1	--	--	--	1
John Scull	1	1	1	1	--	7
Jasper Scull, Esq'r, sheriff	2	1	2	1	--	8
Christopher Smith, butcher	1	1	--	--	--	1
John Schreit, gunsmith	1	1/2	1	1	--	4
Geo. Snyder, mason	1	1	--	1	--	2
James Starr, brewer	1	2	1	1	--	20
John Shorb, shopkeeper	1	1	--	1	--	2
Henry Settely, farmer	--	--	2	1	--	19
Nicholas Shoppert	1	1	--	2	--	1
Thomas Straub	1	1	--	1	--	1

Reading Town	Houses	Lots	Horses	Cattle	Sheep	Tax
Andrew Shauber	1	1	--	1	--	2
Geo. Seitzzinger, b'smith	1	1	1	1	--	4
Fred'k Sensel	1	1	--	--	--	4
George Schultz, hatter & constable	1	1	1	1	--	8
Godlieb Strowhecker, labourer	1	1	--	1	--	1
Valentine Urletig, clock maker	1	1	--	2	--	2
Henry Wolf, shopkeeper	1	1	--	--	--	4
Peter Weiser, sadler	2	2	--	--	--	4
Sam'l Weiser, clerk	1	1/2	--	1	--	5
Jacob Winter, labourer	--	--	--	1	--	1
Isaac Wickersham, joiner & goaler	1	1/2	1	1	--	8
Christ'r Witman, taverner & coroner	2	2	1	1	--	10
Adam Witman, storekeeper & representative	1	2	1	1	--	30
Henry Witman, shoemaker	1	1	1	--	--	1
Francis Wenrich, gent.	1	2	1	1	--	8
Philip Weis, joiner	1	1	--	1	--	2
Geo. Wunder, carpenter	1	1	1	1	--	3
James Whitehead, att'y at law, clerk to com'rs	2	4 3/4	--	2	--	20
Martin Young	1	1	--	1	--	1
Elias Youngman, hatter	1	1/2	1	1	--	4
Isaac Young, storekeeper	1	1	1	1	--	5
Francis Yarnal, mason	1	2	--	--	--	3
Anthony Zimerman	--	--	--	--	--	--

Single Men

	Shillings		Shillings
Adam Diem	15	Jno. Sourmilk	15
Henry Beyerley	15	James Grinding	15
Philip Kreamer	15	John Wessner	15
Thomas Diem	15	Philip Filbert	15
Martin Boyer	15	Casper Potteicher	15
Jacob Oswald	15	Adam Housholder	15
Nicho's Scherer	15	John Kuhn	15
John Brintz	15	Andrew Diem	15
Francis Murray	15	Henry Wolf	15
John Huling	15	Mich'l Marge	15
Wm. Paine	15	Thos. Barger	15
Conrad Geis	15	John Spoon	15
Wm. Grinding	15	Wm. Reener	15
Jeremiah Paul	15	Christ'r Wunder	15
Sam'l Madery	15	John Wolff	15

Rockland Township

	Acres	Horses	Cattle	Sheep	Tax
John Angstadt	212	3	2	--	4
John Albrecht	74	2	2	2	3
John Brem	70	2	1	2	1
John Becher	42	1	2	2	2

Rockland Township

	Houses	Lots	Horses	Cattle	Sheep	Tax
Philip Berlinger	123	2	2	--		5
Jacob Baral	69	1	2	--		2
Nicho Berlinger	140	2	1	--		6
Valentine Bauersack	57	1	1	--		2
W'm Bott, Sen'r	47	2	2	--		2
Nicholas Clementz, g.m.	30	--	1	--		3
John Bott, g.m., s.m.	136	2	4	--		20
Nicholas Dell	30	1	1	--		1
Jacob Drey	150	2	2	--		3
Geo. Drey, labourer	--	--	--	--		1
John Deh, labourer	--	--	--	--		1
Henry Dilbone	250	2	4	4		8
John Ebner	62	2	1	--		1
Jacob Elinger	36	1	1	--		1
Herman Emrich, labourer	--	--	--	--		1
Nicholas Emrich	58	1	--	--		2
Peter Edel	125	1	1	--		2
Peter Ernst, carpenter	--	--	--	--		1
John Fus	30	--	1	--		1
William Folck	85	2	1	2		2
Geo. Falck	74	2	2	--		3
Jacob Henry, labourer	--	--	--	--		1
Jacob Harman	--	1	--	--		2
George Heghst	25	1	2	--		1
Richard Hoffman	70	1	2	--		2
Henry Hoffman	86	2	2	--		5
Andreas Haak, g.m.	7	3	--	--		6
Christian Henry	146	2	2	2		4
Geo. Haffner, jr.	110	2	2	2		3
Jacob Haffner	150	2	2	4		4
Geo. Heffer	175	3	3	4		8
Peter Heider	58	1	1	--		2
Jacob Joder	217	--	--	--		13
Nicho's Jacoby	74	1	2	--		3
Han Nich's Kin	26	--	1	--		1
Samuel Keim, wheelwright	89	1	1	--		4
Christophel Kolb, labourer	--	--	--	--		1
Jacob Keim, turner	126	2	3	--		9
George Kolb	152	2	3	6		2
Leonard Klotz	48	1	2	2		2
And's Kerchner	126	2	3	2		3
Peter Kemb, labourer	--	--	--	--		1
Mich'l Kerwer	12	1	1	--		1
Peter Keffer	295	3	3	--		7
Peter Lobach, f.m.	188	3	4	8		10
Bastian Lentz	140	3	3	--		4
Nicho's Lang, weaver	27	--	1	--		2
Mich'l Lang	75	2	2	2		3
Peter Folck	61	1	1	--		2
John Mack	--	--	--	--		1
Nicho's Meier	75	1	1	--		3
Leonard Miller	146	2	2	--		4
Henry Mertz, s.m.	148	3	3	2		8
Jacob Miller, blacksmith	60	1	2	--		2
George Oberdorff, weaver	42	1	1	--		2

Rockland Township	Houses	Lots	Horses	Cattle	Sheep	Tax
John Rauenzamer, labourer	--	--	--	--		1
Conrad Rauenzamer, labourer	--	--	--	--		1
Casper Rupert	74	2	1	--		1
Casper Reb	64	2	1	--		2
Ludwig Rawenzahner	61	1	2	--		2
Peter Reiff, Jun'r, labourer	--	--	--	--		1
Christian Rieff, potter	52	1	2	--		3
Peter Rieff, Sen'r	498	3	6	2		35
Conrad Schedy	73	1	1	--		2
Michael Sadler, labourer	--	--	--	--		1
Dieder Scheffer	77	1	1	--		4
Martin Schnider	62	2	1	--		2
Valentine Sterner, s.m.	57	1	2	--		3
Michael Sheffer, b. smith	206	2	3	4		10
Casper Seibert, g.m., s.m.	106	1	1	4		10
Henry Sowash	150	2	2	4		8
Casper Weiser, mason	54	1	1	4		1
Lazarus Weidner	50	--	--	--		3
Geo. Zweiger	93	2	2	--		2

Single Men

	Shillings		Shillings
Peter Angstadt	15	Anthony Hefner	15
Dennis Hendley	15	Fred'k Heffner	15
Conrad Reb	15	Dewald Lentz	15
Geo. Barrel	15	Joseph Sweiger	15
Jacob Folck	15	George Kolp	15
Jacob Mertz	15		

Ruscomb Manor Township

	Acres	Horses	Cattle	Sheep	Tax
Adam Anstatt, g.m.	102	1	2	3	5
Joseph Algeiger	33	2	1	3	2
John Albrecht, tile maker	33	--	1	--	1
Jacob Backer	63	1	1	--	2
Joseph Bacher	--	1	1	--	3
Fred'k Bachman	63	3	1	2	2
Christian Bachman	63	2	1	1	3
George Brown, weaver	21	--	1	--	2
John Bower, weaver	60	--	2	--	2
Jacob Berstler	--	1	--	--	3
Margaret Backer	60	3	1	--	1
Jacob Dalman	49	1	2	--	2
Michael Dunckle	60	--	--	--	2
George Emmert, innkeeper	43	2	1	--	3
John Erman, joiner	--	--	1	--	1
Dieter Fahl	205	3	4	6	10
Jacob Fux	108	2	3	2	3
Michael Fisher	35	2	1	2	2

7

Ruscomb Manor Township	Houses	Lots	Horses	Cattle	Sheep	Tax
Ludwig Frantz	35		2	2	--	2
Jacob Gith	88		--	--	--	2
Peter Gidleman	105		--	--	--	2
Jeremias Hess, blacksmith	--		--	1	--	1
X'n Huffnaugle, taylor	90		3	3	6	2
Michael Hensel	50		--	--	--	1
Stephen Haberacre	107		2	2	3	5
Adam Hamshar, weaver	43		--	1	--	2
Peter Heckman	102		2	1	--	2
Jacob Helm	105		3	2	2	3
Dewald Hinter	110		--	2	--	3
Peter Kline	106		2	2	3	2
John Kelchner	108		3	3	4	3
Adam Kehly	--		--	1	--	1
Henry Lautensleger	--		1	--	--	4
Jacob Lippert	200		3	4	3	6
John Lutz	18		1	1	--	1
Henry Miller	168		2	1	2	3
George Michael	--		--	1	--	1
Gaby Martin	--		--	1	--	1
Tobias Metzger	--		--	1	--	1
Conrad Price	210		3	4	8	13
Jacob Roller	--		2	1	--	1
John Rey	--		--	--	--	1
John Riegle	64		2	2	2	2
Michael Rettinger	35		--	1	--	2
George Rack, innkeeper	188		3	4	2	7
Engle Roether	--		--	1	--	1
Adam Rauzahn	50		1	1	--	2
Michael Spang	--		--	1	--	1
Adam Spittlemyer	103		1	1	--	2
Andreas Swartz	51		1	1	--	2
Peter Shumaker	--		1	--	--	1
Christ'r Sheth	45		2	1	--	2
Adam Schmael	108		2	3	4	5
Michael Siegfried, tyler	95		4	2	--	4
Jacob Sammet	--		--	--	--	2
George Silver	--		2	1	--	1
Geo. Swartz	--		--	--	--	1
Peter William	135		2	3	4	4
Jost. Wagner	155		4	4	8	9
Dieter Welcker	500		--	--	--	25
John Wescow	51		--	1	--	2
Jacob Zanger, s.m., g.m.	53		2	2	--	5
Peter Zimmerman	--		--	1	--	3
Ludwig Sherk	--		--	1	--	1
X'n Rodarmal	50		--	--	--	1
X'r Teisher	50		--	--	--	2
Peter Rodarmal	50		--	--	--	2
Elias Reed	20		--	--	--	1

Single Men

	Shillings		Shillings
John Oseas	15	Jacob Miller	15
Adam Lippert	15	John Miller	15
David Foll	15	Peter Wanner	15
Dieter Fahl	15	Bastian Fucks	15

Colebrookdale Township

	Acres	Horses	Cattle	Sheep	Tax
Peter Allenbach, farmer	200	2	4	4	10
Conrad Bear, farmer	122	2	6	4	4
Jacob Bohm, farmer	172	3	3	3	4
Andrew Brendle, Sen'r, farmer	--	1	1	--	2
Casper Bowman, farmer	118	--	--	--	2
Martin Bealer, farmer	--	--	--	--	1
John Buckwalder, farmer	290	4	7	7	15
Casper Bucher, farmer	130	4	4	6	5
Peter Botty, farmer	--	--	1	--	1
Nicholas Eiss, farmer	223	4	12	5	11
Frederick Earney, farmer	120	2	4	--	5
Henry Engle, farmer	202	3	3	--	18
Christian Eschbach	50	--	--	--	2
Mary Eshenback, widow	210	3	3	7	3
William Engle, labourer	--	--	1	--	1
Godfredt Feyck, shoemaker	--	--	2	--	1
John French, farmer	75	2	3	2	2
Michael Fertig, taylor	27	1	2	--	2
Adam Fucks, farmer	212	4	4	4	12
Philip Fryman	--	--	1	--	1
Joseph Fox, & Co.	2,000	--	--	--	55
Adam Fox	208	--	--	--	5
Joacam Gotschalk, farmer	109	2	1	3	3
Geo. John Getz, miller	--	1	2	--	3
George Gilbert, farmer	150	3	4	6	6
Adam Gerber, farmer	36	2	2	4	3
John Gerber, farmer	138	2	3	5	8
George Hartman, labourer	--	1	2	--	3
John Guldin, farmer, s.m.	252	3	4	1	16
Leonard Gerber, farmer	--	--	1	--	1
John Heltman, blacksmith	206	1	3	--	1
Jacob Herth, farmer	135	2	2	--	5
Michael Jerger, farmer	75	2	2	--	5
Michael Huntzer	--	--	--	--	1
Stephen Krumrine, farmer	300	5	6	6	15
Michael Kusser, farmer	152	3	3	6	6
David Kepler, potter	70	2	4	3	5
Jacob Kruss, miller, g.m.	25	2	1	3	2
John Koch, farmer	133	3	3	4	4
Peter Loeg, farmer	164	4	5	4	8
Peter Levegood, founder	--	1	1	--	1
George Landes, farmer	142	4	4	4	6
Peter Lober, farmer	200	4	7	4	9
Jacob Meisenhamer, farmer	24	4	4	--	13

9

Colebrookdale Township	Acres	Horses	Cattle	Sheep	Tax
Jacob Mechlin, farmer	236	4	12	--	11
Stophel Moll, waggoner	100	3	3	1	4
Tobias Mauck, farmer	118	3	5	6	3
Elizabeth Moyer	50	--	--	--	2
Daniel Pheil, farmer	53	1	1	--	5
Thomas Ruther, Esq'r, g.m., s.m.	575	6	12	5	40
Martin Rupp	--	--	--	--	1
Math's Roads, j'r, farmer	212	4	7	9	13
Mat's Roads, Sen'r, farmer	201	4	6	6	7
Casper Richard, farmer	317	4	6	17	16
Adam Road, farmer, g.m., s.m.	128	2	4	3	8
Paul Ritter, farmer	318	4	8	5	18
John Stouffer, farmer	25	--	--	--	1
Earhard Stohl, farmer	--	--	--	--	1
Jacob Smith, farmer	154	3	4	--	6
Geo. Swinehard, farmer	158	3	5	5	11
Geo. Snep, labourer	--	1	1	3	1
Abram Stouber, Sen'r, farmer	200	2	4	3	13
Andreas Swinehard, miller, g.m.	55	--	2	--	5
Manus Sasamanhous, farmer	234	4	6	6	22
Cha's Safred	100	--	--	--	2
John Sleichger, labourer	--	--	--	--	1
Henry Schrem, labourer	76	2	2	--	6
Nicholas Smith, labourer	91	1	2	2	2
Abraham Stauber, j'r, farmer	199	4	3	4	7
Peter Schaen, farmer, g.m.	136	3	4	6	6
Thomas Schaen, farmer	128	2	2	--	3
Jacob Seibert, farmer	--	--	1	--	1
Baltzer Trout, farmer	4	1	1	--	2
Thomas West, labourer	--	--	1	--	1
John Werstler, farmer	111	3	6	6	6

Single Men

	Shillings
Fredrick Richard	15
Mathias Ritter	15
John Earney	15

Richmond Township

	Acres	Horses	Cattle	Sheep	Tax
Anthony Adam	100	2	2	3	6
Geo. Angstad	--	--	--	--	6
Henry Burgardt	50	2	2	--	2
Peter Beel	100	3	3	--	11
Melchior Brown	25	--	--	--	2
John Berto	90	2	2	--	3
Nicholas Bever	50	2	2	--	3
John Patton, Esq'r, g.m., s.m.	150	--	--	--	27
Jacob Deisher	260	3	4	2	15
Nicholas Ely	100	3	2	--	3

Richmond Township	Acres	Horses	Cattle	Sheep	Tax
Abram Dreiblebiss	200	3	6	4	10
Casper Dom	60	1	1	--	2
Christ'r Deischer	150	3	4	4	14
Henry Erdle	150	2	1	2	6
Elizabeth Ely	250	3	4	6	10
George Foulk	100	2	2	3	5
Valentine Gress	100	--	1	--	2
Peter Greenwald	150	2	3	5	6
John Glass	100	3	2	2	5
Mich'l Gollinger	100	2	2	--	4
Henry Heavener	150	3	2	3	10
Michael Hessler	50	1	1	--	1
Jacob Heavely	100	2	2	6	3
Michael Heavely	50	2	1	--	2
Fredrick Hill	200	4	8	10	22
Daniel High	200	3	3	4	14
John Hager	100	2	3	6	4
Michael Henzel	100	3	2	4	4
John Johnson	400	--	--	--	56
Conrad Kolb	100	2	3	--	3
David Kamp	100	2	2	2	2
Theobald Kiefer	150	3	4	6	11
George Kelchner	200	4	6	7	14
Nicholas Kiefer	200	4	3	6	10
Michael Kantz	60	1	1	--	2
Jacob Lupper	70	2	2	--	3
Geo. Merckel, s.m., g.m.	300	5	12	10	36
Peter Merckel	250	3	10	10	21
Casper Merckel	50	2	2	4	7
Geo. Merckel	100	3	2	3	3
Conrad Miller	150	3	4	3	9
Andreas Millshlegel	70	2	2	3	2
Michael Miller	200	2	2	3	14
Baltzer Moon	100	3	2	4	3
Geo. Nuz	100	2	2	--	3
George Ohl	100	2	1	2	3
Adolph Peter	100	3	1	2	3
Michael Reber	100	3	2	4	4
John Resler	100	2	2	3	2
John Rothermal	200	--	--	--	5
Baltzer Riehm	150	3	3	4	8
George Rack	150	2	4	2	12
Anthony Schretter	100	2	2	2	3
Geo. Scheffer	150	3	3	4	9
Christian Schick	160	2	2	4	3
Peter Spoohn	100	2	2	--	3
Philip Soons	50	2	2	3	2
Urban Sheadle	50	3	2	--	2
John Slegle	100	3	3	5	5
Michael William	50	2	2	2	2
Jacob Wanner	100	3	2	3	7
Conrad Brendlinger	--	--	--	--	1
Nicholas Beron	--	--	--	--	1
Fredrick Bauer	--	--	--	--	1
Fredrick Brown	--	--	--	--	3

Richmond Township	Acres	Horses	Cattle	Sheep	Tax
George Beigler	--	--	--	--	1
Michael Boabst	--	--	--	--	1
Henry Chrisman	--	--	--	--	2
Peter Dilbone	25	--	--	--	2
Abraham Ely	--	--	--	--	1
Mich'l Knittel	--	--	--	--	1
Daniel Kleim	--	--	--	--	1
Peter Moon	--	--	--	--	1
Ludwig Aderman	--	--	--	--	1
George Rab	--	--	--	--	1
Geo. Springer	20	--	--	--	1
Peter Shible	--	--	--	--	1

Single Men

	Shillings		Shillings
Christ'r Baur	15	John Ely	15
John Camber	15	Geo. Kreff	15
Abram Dreibelpis	15	Lon'd Messersmith	15
Jacob Dedweiler	15	Joseph Miethhard	15

Albany Township

	Acres	Horses	Cattle	Sheep	Tax
George Arnold	100	2	2	2	2
Michael App	30	--	--	--	1
Jacob Bacher	100	2	1	2	2
Nicholas Bacher	100	2	2	2	4
George Mich'l Breyner, s.m.	100	4	4	6	18
Ann Eliz'a Broabst, 2 g. & s.m.'s	100	2	4	4	9
Michael Broabst, g.m.	200	4	3	4	12
Daniel Baushar	100	2	2	--	2
Arnold Billig	100	2	2	--	4
Frantz Belly	100	2	2	3	2
Michael Breinig	--	--	1	--	1
Martin Bernheisel	--	--	1	--	1
Geo. Bauman	--	--	1	--	1
Christ'r Braucher	--	2	2	--	2
Valentine Delb	--	--	--	--	1
George Drum	50	2	1	2	3
Jacob Dress	--	--	1	--	1
Jacob Donat	30	1	1	--	2
Francis Frey	--	--	1	--	1
Wm. Farmer	100	2	2	1	3
Martin Forsch	--	--	1	--	1
Jacob Gortner	100	2	2	2	4
Peter Gortner	100	2	1	2	2
Jacob Gerhard	100	2	2	--	3
Christian Henry	100	2	2	2	5
George Haal	150	2	2	3	3
John Hayn	75	2	2	2	3
George Hand	100	2	1	--	3

12

Albany Township	Acres	Horses	Cattle	Sheep	Tax
Frederick Hauer	98	3	2	3	6
Michael Herbster	150	1	2	3	5
Andreas Hagenbuch	150	3	3	3	9
Henry Hagenbach	--	--	1	--	1
Christian Hegler	200	3	4	6	10
George Kungle	100	2	2	2	5
Bernhard Kreamer	--	--	--	--	1
Peter Kneper, Sen'r	100	2	2	3	3
Geo. Kautzman	--	2	1	--	2
Jacob Kuns	100	2	2	2	5
John Korrel	100	3	2	4	4
Peter Kneper, Jr.	150	2	3	4	4
John Klick	100	2	2	3	3
Adam Kreitz	--	--	1	--	1
John Kistler	100	2	3	4	4
John Kreitz	100	2	2	2	3
Peter Klingemen	150	2	2	2	4
Martin Kamp	100	2	2	--	4
Jacob Lantz	150	2	2	4	5
Nicho's Lambert, g.m.	100	2	2	2	7
George Lilly	100	4	3	4	5
John Mayer	20	--	1	--	1
Nich's Miltenberger	66	2	2	2	3
Mich'l Maurer	95	2	1	--	3
Geo. Mich'l Miller	100	2	2	2	3
Jacob Neyford	--	--	1	--	1
Henry Nerhud	100	2	1	--	2
Jacob Poh	100	2	1	2	3
Valentine Petry	100	2	2	--	2
Hen. Reichelsderffer	50	2	2	--	4
Geo. Riegle	50	--	1	2	2
John Reinhard	100	2	2	3	3
Ferdinandt Ritter	200	--	2	3	3
Barbara Ritter	300	4	4	4	10
Christ'r Rentzberger	50	2	1	--	2
Peter Sebold	50	1	1	--	1
Geo. Scherff	50	--	1	--	1
Christ'r Scherff	--	--	1	--	1
Anthony Shaller	50	2	1	1	2
John Stiegewald	50	2	2	3	3
Peter Spengler, g.m.	100	--	2	--	5
Henry Schweng	--	--	1	--	1
Geo. Sweng	150	2	2	2	1
Daniel Smith	100	--	--	--	4
Nicho's Strasser	150	3	2	2	5
Wm. Stump	150	3	4	5	5
Jacob Stam	50	1	2	2	1
Geo. Smetter	--	--	1	--	1
Philip Shellhamer	--	--	1	--	1
Nicholas Smith	50	2	1	2	4
Jacob Smith	50	--	1	--	1
Tobias Stapleton	200	4	4	5	9
Cornelius Freese, dec'd	150	--	--	--	3
Mich'l Werlin, 2 s. & g.m.'s	100	3	2	5	7
Jacob Werth	100	--	1	2	2

Albany Township	Acres	Horses	Cattle	Sheep	Tax
John Wesner	50	--	1	--	1
John Zimerman	--	--	1	--	1
Henry Zimerman	100	2	2	2	2

Single Men

	Shillings		Shillings
Jacob Hagabuch	15	George Kungel	15
Adam Staller	15	Henry Fager	15
John Stabelton	15	Jacob Stump	15
Daniel Riegel	15		

Bethel Township

	Acres	Horses	Cattle	Sheep	Tax
Christian Bardorf	100	2	2	2	5
Henry Bardorf	50	2	1	--	3
Henry Berger	100	2	2	2	4
George Berger	100	2	2	1	2
George Beshore	108	3	4	7	5
Jacob Beshore	100	1	--	--	2
Hanes Borcket	100	1	1	1	2
Emanuel Borcket	50	2	2	1	1
Peter Bucksler	200	2	3	3	5
Peter Bucksler, Jun'r	100	2	2	2	2
Jacob Bortner	50	2	2	4	3
Isaiah Cushwa	50	--	--	--	2
Ludwig Derr	200	2	2	2	12
Adam Daniel	50	2	2	--	4
Jacob Emrich	100	2	2	--	3
John Emrich	50	2	2	2	3
George Emmert	100	2	2	3	6
John Gungel	100	2	6	2	7
Nicho's Gebhart	50	2	2	2	3
Philip Gundrum	50	2	3	--	2
Christ'r Herold	50	2	2	--	4
Peter Hefli	50	2	2	--	2
Phil. Lorentz Hautz	150	2	4	3	10
Philip Hautz	100	1	1	--	2
Henry Kobel	100	1	1	--	2
Wendel Kueffer	100	1	2	1	3
George Kraff	180	2	2	2	3
Peter Klein	50	1	1	--	1
Peter Kreitzer	125	--	--	--	4
Adam Kassel	100	2	2	4	4
Daniel Kabel	100	2	2	--	2
Geo. Michael Kraff	50	1	1	--	2
Christopher Knebel	100	2	3	3	6
Wm. Krichbaum	100	2	3	1	2
John Kremmer	50	1	3	1	2
Daniel Kremmer, s.m.	30	--	1	--	2
John Korngibel	30	2	1	--	2

Bethel Township	Acres	Horses	Cattle	Sheep	Tax
Baltzer Lesch	100	2	2	--	4
Nicholas Mercki	100	3	3	5	2
David Mercki	150	3	3	5	1
George Munch	100	2	2	2	2
John Meyer	100	2	2	3	6
Peter Meyer	100	2	2	2	4
Leonard Miller, s.m.	200	2	2	2	11
Miller Michael	150	2	2	4	5
Christ'r Neicomer, s.m.	170	4	4	4	7
Martin Oberle	100	1	1	--	2
Nicholas Puntzuis	50	2	2	2	4
Christ'r Paffenberger	100	2	2	--	2
John Peiffer	--	1	1	--	1
Jacob Schwab	50	1	1	--	1
Daniel Schneider	100	2	2	2	5
Dietrich Sicks	100	1	2	--	3
John Strubhauer	100	1	1	--	1
Henry Stumb	100	1	1	--	2
Geo. Adam Stumb	50	1	1	--	2
John Schuy	60	2	2	2	3
Casper Schnebele	150	2	5	--	7
Charles Smith	50	1	1	--	1
Adam Smith	50	1	1	--	2
Martin Schuy	200	3	3	2	5
Jacob Schott	100	2	2	2	2
Peter Schmidt	100	2	1	--	2
Lorentz Sambel	100	2	2	--	1
Wendel Seybert, blacksmith	180	6	8	10	12
Hannes Stein	100	2	1	2	5
Leon'd Schwartz	100	2	2	2	7
Jacob Sierrer	100	2	2	--	3
Jacob Tenny	100	2	2	2	4
Mardin Tresster	50	2	2	2	4
Casper Tomas	150	2	5	--	6
Jacob Volmer	40	1	2	2	2
Michael Weiland	150	2	3	4	5
Nicholas Wolf	100	2	6	2	6
Stophell Weitmer	50	2	2	2	4
Lewis Wentzlein	50	1	1	--	1
Christ'n Walbern	25	2	2	--	4
Mich'l Zerben	50	4	2	--	2
Valentine Zerben	--	--	--	--	2
Hanes Frantz	190	2	4	4	6
Stophel Reier	100	2	2	3	7
Geo. Reitz	100	1	1	--	6
John Reis	100	--	--	--	5

Single Men

	Shillings		Shillings
Daniel Bicksler	15	Peter Denger	15
Michael Wolff	15	Hannes Becksler	15
Leonard Lemmer	15		

Labourers

	Pounds		Pounds
Andreas Emrich	1	Jacob Ferst	1
Geo. Jung	1	Jacob Spies	1
John Gunkel	1	Leonard Kro	1
Henry Kehler	1	Peter Schwartz	1
Han Kobel	1	Wilhelm Weis	1
Henry Gilman	1		

Carnarvon Township

	Acres	Horses	Cattle	Sheep	Tax
William Boice, farmer	200	5	3	5	12
Mark Beeler, farmer	100	2	2	5	6
Mathias Broadsword, farmer	100	2	2	3	2
Jacob Cofman, miller, 2 g. & s.m.'s	12	2	4	--	14
John Elliot, farmer	125	2	2	5	9
John Fair, weaver	100	2	2	4	2
Michael Finfrock, farmer	100	1	2	--	2
Samuel Flower, comp'y	300	--	--	--	30
John Gabriel, constable	200	3	2	2	7
John Goheen, smith	164	2	2	--	8
John Holy, farmer	160	2	2	6	4
Thomas Herper	--	1	1	--	1
John Hudson, farmer	340	--	1	--	5
Jacob Hofman, farmer	60	2	2	1	2
John Jones, inn keeper	180	4	2	4	13
David Jones, farmer	100	4	4	4	7
Jonathan Jones, farmer	200	4	4	10	12
John Light, farmer	150	8	4	15	23
Christian Long, farmer	140	2	2	4	5
Adam Long, farmer	100	1	1	--	2
Dietrich Lefler, sow gelder	100	1	1	3	2
John Minsear	--	1	--	--	1
Jacob Morgan, esquire	300	15	4	86	28
Thomas Morgan, farmer	250	10	4	--	7
Manus Magache, labourer	--	1	--	--	1
Geo Reesor, farmer	200	2	3	4	18
Wm. Robinson, farmer	97	5	1	7	6
John Robinson, farmer	96	--	--	1	2
Joseph Richardson	--	--	--	--	4
Aaron Ratew, farmer	249	6	2	6	8
Wm. Reese, fuller, f.m.	30	2	1	--	7
Darby Sulevan	--	--	1	--	1
Cornelius Shea	--	1	--	--	1
Benjamin Talbot, farmer	50	1	2	4	4
Joseph Talbot, farmer	--	--	--	--	--
William Wells, blacksmith	60	2	1	1	4
James Wells, farmer	160	2	1	1	6
Hugh Wear, b'smith	--	1	1	--	2
Geo. Wilson, farmer	--	--	2	--	1
John Gordon, labourer	--	1	--	--	1
John Dumbar	--	1	--	--	1
Oliver Allen	--	--	--	--	1
Thomas Scott	--	--	--	--	1
George Raysor	--	--	--	--	1

Single Men

	Shillings		Shillings
David Martin	15	Roger Starling	15
Patrick Gordon	15	John Hudson	15
James Sullevan	15	Thomas Morgan	15
Robert Sterling	15	John Robeson	15

Brecknock Township

	Acres	Horses	Cattle	Sheep	Tax
Widow Balzly's	200	2	4	--	--
Bernhard Bealer, farmer	150	2	3	4	--
Adam Boemer, farmer	150	2	3	4	--
Henry Barr, farmer	178	3	5	8	--
Henry Brendle, taylor	50	2	2	--	--
Jacob Frey, farmer	150	2	2	2	--
Michael Frankhouser, farmer	70	2	2	5	--
Christian Geman, wheelwright	100	2	2	2	--
Chas. Hornberger, farmer	100	2	2	3	--
Hans Hemig, weaver	110	2	2	3	--
Geo. Heisung, weaver	150	2	1	--	--
Hans Komler, joiner	40	1	2	--	--
Daniel Kiefer, weaver	81	2	3	3	--
Adam Krick, farmer	100	1	2	--	--
Casper Koch, farmer	100	1	1	--	--
Daniel Komer, farmer	200	1	3	3	--
John Ley, farmer	50	2	2	4	--
Frantz Marshal, farmer	150	--	2	--	--
Martin Minder, farmer	96	1	2	--	--
Hans Moser, farmer	90	--	5	--	--
Henry Miller, farmer	--	--	--	--	--
Jacob Muller, shoemaker	50	1	1	2	--
Adam Neidig, farmer	120	2	5	6	--
Emanuel Peiffer, farmer	50	1	1	--	--
John Pennebaker, f. & s.m., farmer	200	4	5	2	--
Jeremiah Seamer, farmer	200	3	4	8	--
John Thomas Segner, blacksmith	50	2	1	--	--
Michael Schlauch, farmer	50	2	1	--	--
Thomas Scharn, farmer	50	1	3	2	--
Nicholas Jontz, farmer	130	2	6	--	--
Joseph Wanger, farmer	10	--	3	--	--
Jacob Wirt, farmer	100	1	3	--	--
Leopold Jost, farmer	174	3	6	6	--
Fred'k Heminger, farmer	--	--	--	--	--
Adam Gige, farmer	--	--	--	--	--

Single Men

	Shillings		Shillings
Hans Hemich	15	Solomon Neidig	15
Henry Seamer	15	Henry Brendle	15
Fredrick Sweltzer	15	Jacob Komler	15

17

Alsace Township

	Acres	Horses	Cattle	Sheep	Tax
George Braun	--	--	--	--	--
Conrad Bab	150	3	2	--	--
John Baum	190	3	4	6	--
Henry Baum	150	2	3	3	--
Lorentz Beck	--	--	--	--	--
Jacob Becker	70	2	4	--	--
Dieter Beidleman	202	2	4	6	--
Henry Becker	100	2	2	--	--
Jacob Bleiler	70	2	2	--	--
Martin Dressbach	240	2	4	--	--
Daniel Dirck	200	--	--	--	--
Jacob Depree	--	1	--	--	--
Mathias Drinckel	100	2	2	--	--
Valentine Eckert	150	3	5	3	--
John Ebeling	175	2	4	4	--
Nicholas Fischer	250	4	3	4	--
Michael Fischer	180	2	3	3	--
John Fischer	210	2	3	3	--
Christian Feick	60	2	1	2	--
Rudolph Garrett	280	2	3	4	--
Adam Garrett	180	2	2	2	--
Nicholas Grasher	57	1	1	2	--
Adam Geiger	10 1/2	1	--	--	--
Samuel Hoch	270	4	5	5	--
Richard Hockly	100	--	--	--	--
Adam Heckman	170	--	2	--	--
Peter Heckman	--	--	--	--	--
Adam Heckman, j'r	--	--	--	--	--
George Heuer	70	2	2	--	--
John Haveracker	250	3	4	3	--
Michael Hoffman	220	2	2	4	--
Geo. Heist	9	--	1	--	--
Nicholas Jost	207	4	4	5	--
Thomas Jungman	5	1	1	--	--
Michael Jaeig	--	--	--	--	--
Lorentz Krone	120	1	--	--	--
Jacob Kean	180	4	4	--	--
Jacob Kissinger	220	3	2	--	--
John Klose	210	4	3	6	--
Conrad Keller	260	3	3	--	--
Philip Knep	--	--	--	--	--
David Kintzig	200	2	2	4	--
George Keller	220	1	1	--	--
Jacob Landsiscus	150	2	4	5	--
Jacob Lutz	47 1/2	1	1	--	--
Peter Loch	130	--	--	--	--
George Lora	60	2	1	--	--
Thomas Lewis	140	2	3	6	--
Mich'l Maurer	140	2	3	4	--
Mathias Mauty	50	1	1	--	--
Peter Miller	161	2	3	4	--
William Noll	115	2	1	--	--
Daniel Norgang	115	2	1	--	--
Ludwig Riegle	70	2	2	4	--

Alsace Township	Acres	Horses	Cattle	Sheep	Tax
Conrad Roerich	120	2	3	--	--
Adam Rickenbach	260	4	4	3	--
Philip Rieser	130	2	2	--	--
Victor Spiece	140	2	3	2	--
Henry Schaedler	--	--	--	--	--
Conrad Smith	210	2	1	--	--
Henry Scheit	92	2	2	--	--
Philip Sailer	250	2	2	3	--
Christ'r Spengler	260	4	4	4	--
W'm Shepler	104	1	2	--	--
Henry Smith	--	--	--	--	--
Henry Schmeck	200	2	4	5	--
Casper Stroll	130	2	2	6	--
Philip Wentzel	90	2	2	3	--
Philip Wax	120	2	3	--	--
John Wolf	70	1	1	--	--
Jose Walter	--	--	--	--	--
Dan'l Zacharias	200	2	3	3	--

Single Men

	Shillings		Shillings
John Balty	15	Christ'r Kintzy	15
George Spengler	15	Mich'l spoon	15
John Haveracre	15	Geo. Rodenberger	15
Mich'l Becker	15	Jacob Garrett	15
Abraham Kintzy	15		

Cumru Township

	Acres	Horses	Cattle	Sheep	Tax
Jonas Adam	--	--	--	--	1
James Arnet, labourer	--	--	1	--	1
Peter Ashelman	100	2	3	6	8
Lloyd Abel	100	--	--	--	2
Jacob Bechtel, farmer	150	3	2	3	9
Jacob Becht	150	2	1	--	1
Dennis Bready	250	1	1	--	12
John Bugh, taylor	--	--	--	--	1
John Bullman, blacksmith	200	4	2	4	15
Jacob Berck, wagoner	--	--	1	--	1
Henry Binckley	70	2	2	--	2
Martin Breininger	80	1	2	2	2
Christian Binckley, farmer	100	3	3	--	6
Jacob Bauman, s.m.	105	2	4	4	9
Christian Bauman	115	3	4	6	16
Jacob Blessing	50	1	--	--	1
Geo. Burgard	100	1	4	4	4
John Geo. Minter	150	1	1	--	6
John Davis, fuller, f.m.	130	3	5	6	19
Christian Dreat, farmer	100	3	2	12	6
James Davis	150	3	2	--	17

19

Cumru Township	Acres	Horses	Cattle	Sheep	Tax
John Davis	150	3	3	6	12
Thomas Davis	150	2	2	3	15
Jacob Drietch, weaver	50	1	1	--	2
Andreas Deem	100	1	1	--	1
John Dowdrich, farmer	100	3	2	--	9
Geo. Drustel, blacksmith	50	1	1	--	2
Peter Degher, s.m.	100	3	4	6	16
Nathan Evans, g.m.	300	2	3	6	20
Geo. Engelhard, blacksmith	14	1	1	--	4
Samuel Embree	100	3	2	6	12
David Evans	150	3	4	6	18
Nicholas Emmig	100	4	2	6	4
John Engelbrown, farmer	130	3	3	6	1
Joshua Evans	100	2	2	--	18
Samuel Flower	400	--	--	--	40
Mich'l Frymyer	--	--	1	--	1
Mich'l Folmer	100	2	2	--	5
Jacob Frymyer, s.m., g.m.	150	4	3	6	14
Dietrich Fernsler	100	2	2	--	4
Christian Furrer, s.m., g.m.	240	4	4	7	4
John Finscher	100	2	3	2	2
Michael Fetterly	60	2	2	--	2
John Henry Falcky	50	1	--	--	5
George Gebhart	100	--	1	--	4
Joseph Garber	--	--	--	--	1
John Gerber, s.m., g.m.	40	2	2	5	12
James Gibbins	--	--	--	--	1
Philip Gabel	25	1	1	--	2
Nicholas Gauer, taylor	67	2	3	4	5
Adam Gerrich, farmer	150	2	3	--	3
Jacob Hame	150	1	1	--	4
Edward Harry	180	1	3	10	12
Ulrich Houder	60	2	2	--	3
Evan Harry	1	1	2	2	8
Jacob Hauck	250	4	4	4	13
Conrad Hartt	150	--	--	--	13
Mich'l Herold	--	--	--	--	1
Rudolph Heberling, farmer	100	2	3	3	5
Peter Hushar	50	2	2	--	3
Adam Householder	300.	4	4	6	17
W'm Huttenstein	130	3	4	--	24
George Jacob	100	2	3	3	6
Nicholas Jost, g.m.	200	4	2	--	6
James Iddings	--	1	1	--	1
Leon'd Keplinger	100	2	2	--	2
Jacob Kern, s.m.	300	5	6	6	18
George Krick	60	2	2	--	3
Michael Kern	80	2	2	--	3
Jno. Kleinginny, farmer	79	2	2	4	3
X'n Koenig	100	--	1	--	2
Jacob Kurtz, farmer	150	2	3	5	10
Jacob Koch	100	4	2	--	5
And's Kockel	150	3	4	--	6
Conrad Krichbaum	50	1	1	--	2
Mich'l Keyser, farmer	180	4	4	4	12

Cumru Township	Acres	Horses	Cattle	Sheep	Tax
Francis Kreek, Sen'r	150	4	4	6	16
Francis Kreek, j'r, shoemaker	--	--	1	--	1
John Krick	80	2	2	2	4
Jacob Kreek, blacksmith	--	--	1	--	3
Conrad Landsdorff	--	--	1	--	1
Nathan Lewis	150	2	3	2	12
William Lewis	150	4	3	4	12
Mich'l Leonard	100	1	1	--	2
Michael Lapp, farmer	120	3	4	7	7
James Lewis	150	4	4	6	13
Richard Lewis	100	4	4	6	10
John Laub	30	--	1	2	2
Mich'l Laub	60	2	2	2	4
Jacob Mechlin	8-	--	--	--	2
Nich's Martsower, s.m.	130	1	--	--	6
Geo. Meyer	1,000	2	2	5	55
Henry Meyer	--	--	--	--	1
Geo. Mycriss, weaver	60	1	2	2	2
Ludwig Moone	400	3	4	--	20
Vernon Moone	--	--	--	--	1
Christian Miller	100	2	2	--	3
Jacob Mishler	--	2	2	--	2
Joseph Mishler	--	2	2	--	2
Christian Maurer, p.m.	30	1	2	--	16
Michael Moyer	50	1	2	--	3
Jno. Morris, heirs	250	4	5	--	16
Jacob Minnig	100	2	1	--	2
Abram Neidig	150	2	3	3	15
David Neidig, blacksmith	50	1	3	2	3
Sam'l Overholtz	70	1	1	--	2
Jacob Remff	50	1	1	--	1
Peter Rufner	50	1	--	--	2
George Riehm, innholder	1 1/2	1	2	--	10
John Riehm	90	--	--	--	2
Jacob Reeser	180	4	3	4	16
Peter Road, g.m.	300	5	6	12	30
Jacob Road	150	4	5	6	18
Michael Road	150	4	6	6	18
Geo. Road	--	1	1	--	4
Hartman Rule	--	1	1	--	3
Ulrich Reish	100	2	3	--	4
John Ruchty, farmer	100	2	2	2	4
Nicholas Scull	--	1	2	--	--
Isaac Sailer, shopkeeper	--	1	1	--	3
Michael Schauer	100	2	2	--	9
Fred'k Shelleberger	50	1	1	--	1
Jonas Seely, Esq'r	700	9	6	--	35
Peter Shearman	100	2	3	--	4
David Smith, farmer	100	3	2	6	6
Jost Shonour	50	2	2	2	2
Christ'n Speicher	138	2	2	4	6
Melchior Steel	50	2	2	--	2
Baltzer Seibert	50	1	1	--	1
John Sullevan	100	1	1	--	1
Philip Spath	50	--	1	--	2

Cumru Township	Acres	Horses	Cattle	Sheep	Tax
Henry Seidenbender	50	1	1	1	2
Henry Spooh	150	3	2	--	10
Hazael Thomas	70	1	1	--	6
Jacob Weis	150	3	3	5	14
Peter Withington, innkeeper	--	--	1	--	2
Fred'k Weitzel	50	2	2	--	3
Eberhard Weidmeier	--	2	2	2	2
Christopher Weis, farmer	130	3	4	2	6
Ludwig Zwernz	150	2	2	--	3
Adam Ziegler	100	1	2	3	5
Jacob Zinn	50	--	--	--	1
Christian Zug	150	4	3	10	12
John Zerbe, s.m.	50	2	1	--	4
Jonathan Zerbe	100	2	2	--	3

Single Men

	Shillings		Shillings
Daniel Morris	15	John Davis	15
Abram Trostell	15	Peter Ruth	15
John George	15	John Frymier	15
Caleb Davis	15	Rubin Davis	15
Henry Weis	15	Ezekiel Morris	15
George Fetterly	15	Henry Tread	15
David Davis	15	Jacob Hauck	15
Adam Diem	15	Daniel Gicker	15
Sam'l Kockel	15	Henry Frymyer	15
Henry Hart	15	Michael Moyer	15
Geo. Breininger	15	John Root	15

Longswamp Township

	Acres	Horses	Cattle	Sheep	Tax
Nicholas Arnold	30	1	1	--	2
Henry Acre	--	--	--	--	1
Christian Berriger, taylor	--	--	--	--	1
Philip Burger	100	2	2	--	4
Charles Bernhard	50	2	1	2	4
Martin Boger	100	3	4	6	14
Ludwig Bitting	95	2	2	3	6
Henry Bury	100	2	2	2	12
Fred'k Boffenmyer	100	2	2	2	9
Philip Beery, g.m.	100	2	2	2	4
Henry Bollinger	100	3	2	3	10
Fred'k Brown	100	2	2	--	5
Peter Butz	200	2	2	4	12
Theobald Carl	100	2	3	4	5
Fred'k Deis	--	--	--	--	1
Peter Dieter	--	--	--	--	1
Jacob Dresner	--	--	--	--	1
Peter Dickert	--	--	--	--	1
Baltzer Dried	--	--	--	--	1

22

Longswamp Township

	Acres	Horses	Cattle	Sheep	Tax
John Diehl	200	2	3	--	10
Philip Dresher	200	4	3	3	10
Samuel Dormayer	50	2	1	--	3
Bernhard Danner	200	2	3	4	6
Martin Dormayer	--	--	--	--	1
John Drexler	25	--	--	--	1
Philip Doll	--	--	--	--	1
Jacob Donner	100	2	3	4	6
John Donckel	24	--	--	--	2
John Egy	100	2	2	2	4
John Eigner, inn keeper	50	2	2	--	5
Mathias Eigner	50	--	--	--	2
Peter Eigner	25	1	--	--	2
Henry Eigner	100	4	3	6	10
Jacob Fenstermaker	100	2	2	--	4
Wm. Fenstermaker	30	2	--	--	3
John Flamer	75	2	2	--	3
Bernhard Fegely	300	4	3	3	20
Mich'l Fisher	100	2	2	5	3
Joseph Folck	40	2	1	--	3
Phil Fenstermacker	150	3	3	2	10
Adam Gory	100	2	2	--	3
Peter Haas	50	--	--	--	3
Frederick Helwig	200	2	3	3	8
Adam Hartman	30	--	1	--	2
Adam Helmstater	50	1	--	2	2
Geo. Herbst	--	--	--	--	1
Michael Jacob	50	1	2	--	3
Conrad Jager	46	2	2	--	2
Samuel Kirch	30	--	1	--	2
Peter Klein	100	2	2	--	1
Martin Karcher	280	4	3	2	15
Carl Kraus	--	--	--	--	1
Henry Kuntz	--	--	--	--	1
Peter Keinerd	30	--	1	--	2
Theobald Keppel	--	--	--	--	1
Theobald Klein	50	2	1	--	3
Michael Kichely	25	--	--	--	1
Henry Knobloch	40	--	--	--	2
Peter Keyser	70	--	--	--	3
Geo. Kreber	25	--	--	--	1
Mat's Ludwig	50	--	--	--	2
Jacob Lang	50	1	1	--	2
Baltzer Lutz	20	--	1	--	2
Conrad Menges	--	--	--	--	1
John Meiner	100	2	5	--	4
Peter Mertz	225	4	5	3	14
Margaret Mertz	100	1	--	--	1
Jacob Mertz	130	2	2	3	5
Ludwig Neitz	--	--	--	--	1
Mich'l Neitterauer	100	2	2	--	5
Benedict Neidlinger	100	2	2	--	3
Eneas Noel	20	1	2	--	2
Anthony Reish	--	--	--	--	1
Peter Rittler	180	3	2	4	6

Longswamp Township	Acres	Horses	Cattle	Sheep	Tax
Fredrick Romig	100	--	--	--	5
Christian Ruth	60	--	--	--	3
Nicholas Shwartz	300	4	4	8	15
Michael Staal	--	--	--	--	1
Nicho's Shearer	--	--	--	--	1
And'w Shnabel	100	2	1	--	4
Urich Schwenkle	--	--	--	--	1
Adam Shelkop	20	--	1	--	1
Jacob Shenck	20	--	2	--	2
Michael Shmit	50	--	2	--	2
Nicholas Seidle	50	1	1	--	2
Mathias Sam	25	--	1	--	2
Andrew Tack	40	--	--	1	2
Geo. Uhre	100	2	2	--	3
Frederick Weible	50	1	1	--	2
Jonas Weber	100	1	2	--	2
Geo. Walbert	50	--	--	--	2
Jacob Weis	25	--	--	--	1
Adam Zener	--	--	--	--	2

Single Men

	Shillings		Shillings
Philip Bury	15	Jacob Flamer	15
Jacob Borger	15	Jacob Fenstermaker	15
Peter Boger	15	Paul Hertzog	15
Bernhard Danner	15	Adam Howerter	15
Jacob Danner	15	George Klein	15
Michael Diehl	15	John Mertz	15
Peter Eigner	15	Peter Mertz	15
Henry Eigner	15	Philip Mertz	15
John Flamer	15	George Weible	15
Christian Fegely	15		

Oley Township

	Acres	Horses	Cattle	Sheep	Tax
Hans Nich's Alstatt	240	2	2	4	14
Fred'k Bertolet	221	4	5	9	24
Wid'w Bertolet	130	4	5	15	31
Isaac Berto	200	3	5	9	15
Peter Briel, o.m.	240	4	3	4	22
John Bertolet	170	3	6	16	25
Mich'l Brust	--	--	1	--	1
Jacob Brown	--	--	1	--	1
Samuel Cooper	--	--	--	--	--
Wm. Collins	30	--	3	--	3
Peter Cutzemyer	--	2	1	--	3
Andreas Derst	--	1	1	--	1
Andreas Dierolf	--	--	1	--	1
Mordecai Ellis	168	3	4	12	14
Jno. Frederick	30	2	2	4	7

Oley Township	Acres	Horses	Cattle	Sheep	Tax
Hanes Fux	--	--	1	--	1
Jacob Fry	--	--	1	--	--
Christ'r Gehrhart	--	--	1	--	1
Daniel Golden	200	3	5	8	32
Samuel Guy, doctor	200	3	4	6	23
Jacob Gelbach	450	5	4	10	35
Fred'k Hill	--	--	1	--	1
Hans Hoch	220	4	5	12	30
Hans Hilbert, g.m.	120	2	2	5	10
Elias Hufnagle	100	2	3	5	18
Benj'a Hufnagle	93	2	4	4	12
Daniel Hoch	150	5	6	12	42
John Hill	150	4	3	6	14
Peter Harpine	200	3	5	6	26
Jacob Harpine	200	3	3	4	32
Jacob Hausinger	--	--	1	--	1
Hans Huff, wheelwright	--	--	1	--	2
David Harpine	100	2	2	3	5
Jacob Kimler	--	--	1	--	1
Casper Krismer	500	4	6	12	48
Jacob Kaufman	354	4	6	8	27
Geo. Keim	150	3	2	4	14
Michael Knabb	192	4	5	8	32
Sam'l Kenig	150	4	6	10	18
Peter Knab	100	2	3	4	16
Henry Kerst	100	4	4	5	20
Thomas Lee	200	4	5	12	30
Jacob Leinbach	150	1	2	--	10
John Lesher, f.	400	8	8	30	100
John Libbert	--	--	1	--	1
Samuel Lee, s.m.	200	4	8	20	35
Henry Leinbach	200	4	4	8	18
Fredrick Lees	--	2	3	--	--
Henry Lees	--	2	3	--	4
John Lee	300	4	10	15	14
Fred'k Leinbach, taylor	--	2	2	--	1
Nicho's Lesher	150	5	5	15	14
Jost Lerk, Shoemaker	--	--	1	--	1
Daniel Levan	135	5	6	15	30
Fred'k Meiner	75	2	2	--	8
Ludwig Marburger	--	--	--	--	1
Henry Minker, hammerman	--	--	--	--	1
Ulrich Mohn, weaver	40	2	2	--	3
Mathias Maser, carpenter	--	--	1	--	1
Peter Michael	--	--	1	--	1
Hanes Mertz, wheelwright	--	--	1	--	1
Melchior Mourer	--	--	1	--	2
Peter Miller	--	--	1	--	1
Jacob Meiner	--	--	--	--	1
Henry Neikerigh, Jr., weaver	--	--	2	--	2
Henry Neikerigh, Sr., weaver	200	3	5	6	12
Jacob Naugle, shoemaker	--	--	--	--	1
Fesper Nain	100	--	2	--	2
Abraham Peter	300	4	4	5	36
Jacob Reider	130	4	3	4	7

Oley Township	Acres	Horses	Cattle	Sheep	Tax
Wm. Reider, cooper	--	--	1	--	1
Christ'r Rodarmel	150	2	3	1	13
Daniel Rodarmel	100	3	2	3	15
Conrad & Son Reiff	900	5	7	18	94
Daniel Reiff	--	2	4	--	6
John Ross, f.	100	--	--	--	14
Moses Roberts	100	1	2	--	6
Wid. & Son Reiser	100	2	2	3	2
Jam's Richardson	--	--	--	--	1
Hannes Stitzel	150	2	5	4	5
Wm. Stapleton	205	3	4	7	18
Jacob Snyder	230	4	5	8	34
Martin Shinkle	500	4	4	15	46
John Shiffer	140	3	5	8	8
Daniel Swartz	--	--	2	--	2
Hen Sleich	100	3	4	6	10
George Swartz, taylor	--	2	1	--	2
Henry Smith, tanner	--	1	1	--	5
Geo. Swope	--	--	--	--	1
Jacob Shoch	--	--	--	--	1
Mat's Sourmilk, b'smith	25	--	1	--	2
Lorentz Speler	--	--	1	--	1
John Terck	300	5	6	12	48
Techims Weldner	100	3	4	10	16
Jacob Weist, Sen'r	100	3	4	--	8
Jacob Weist, Jr.	--	--	--	--	1
Dieter Welker, f.	70	4	--	--	15
Dan'l Wensel, shoemaker	70	1	1	--	2
Lazarus Weidner	125	4	5	8	20
David Weiser	200	4	6	10	25
Martin Wetzel	--	--	--	--	2
George Welde	--	--	1	--	1
Jacob Wesner	--	--	--	--	2
John Witman, inn keeper	--	1	1	--	3
Anthony Yeager, g. & s.m.	400	6	6	8	60
John Yeager, inn keeper	118	2	3	8	29
Mich'l Yoder, g.m.	--	4	3	3	15
Jno. Jost Yoder	150	5	4	10	21
Sam'l Yoder	100	2	2	4	12
Jacob & John Yoder, Jr.	200	3	4	4	28
Peter Yoder	100	4	5	15	20

Single Men

	Shillings		Shillings
John Barrel	15	Mich'l Rapp	15
Peter Breifogle	15	Max Schiffer	15
Daniel Bertolet	15	Martin Scheffer	15
Hanes Beckley	15	Jacob Sylvius	15
Samuel Guldin	15	Jacob Shenck	15
Francis Huffnagle	15	Fred'ker Sourbeer	15
Hans Hercher	15	Henry Sleicher	15
Philip Kaup	15	John Thomas	15

Single Men

	Shillings		Shillings
Jacob Kelchner	15	John Thomas	15
Abraham Kestenholtz	15	John Teater	15
Isaac Levan	15	Christian Weiser	15
Andreas Lerck	15	Daniel Yeager	15
Sam'l Messersmith	15	Jacob Yoder	15
Dan'l Manmiller	15	John Scheffer	15
Hans Neinkirch	15	Jacob Gelbach	15
Peter Nargang	15	David Harpine	15
Alex'r Pilgram	15	Fesper Nein	15
Peter Read	15	David Reis	15

Maxatawny Township

	Acres	Horses	Cattle	Sheep	Tax
Anthony Aldman, tanner	50	1	1	--	2
Michael Andrew, taylor	100	2	2	--	2
Nicholas Bader, shoemaker	15	1	1	--	2
Mich'l Bauer	250	3	3	4	8
John Bast	200	4	4	5	14
John Beaver	150	2	3	4	14
Detors Bever	330	4	4	8	13
Jacob Bever, shoemaker	100	--	2	--	4
Ulrich Bruner	75	2	1	--	3
Conrad Bader	150	4	3	4	11
Theobald Beaver	150	3	4	4	14
Sebald Bader, blacksmith	--	--	1	--	1
Christian Baum	--	2	2	3	2
Peter Braun, taylor	20	1	1	--	2
Valentine Christ, b'smith	--	--	2	--	1
Mich'l Christman	200	5	4	6	17
Peter Classmayer	--	--	1	--	1
Mich'l Classer	100	2	2	2	5
Fred'k Delaplank	900	--	--	--	30
Henry Dorr	200	3	4	4	8
Valentine Emrich	--	1	1	2	1
Geo Esser	--	--	1	--	1
Anthony Fisher	180	3	3	3	8
John Hill	200	4	6	10	10
Mich'l Heninger, potter	200	1	1	1	7
Nicholas Hermany	300	4	4	8	19
David Hottenstein	350	4	6	--	40
Jacob Hartman	100	3	2	--	5
Andrew Haak	200	4	4	5	15
Philip Heyman	--	--	1	--	1
Philip Hen, smith	100	1	1	--	4
Fred'k Houseman, b'smith	200	4	4	4	10
Jacob Koenig, shoemaker	--	1	2	--	1
Geo. Kumb	--	2	1	--	1
Theobald Krub	--	1	1	--	1
George Kootz	250	4	4	--	26
Charles Korn	100	--	2	--	2
Jacob Kumb	--	--	1	--	1
Melchior Kloss	--	--	1	--	1

Maxatawny Township	Acres	Horses	Cattle	Sheep	Tax
Jacob Kutz	100	5	5	8	28
Nicho's Kutz	177	4	4	3	20
Adam Kutz	120	4	5	--	13
John Krumbach	--	1	--	--	1
Jacob Lang	--	--	1	--	1
Michael Lang	200	4	4	4	13
Henry Lutz, weaver	--	--	1	--	1
John Long	173	4	3	3	14
Jacob Levan	300	4	6	10	36
Daniel Levan, taverner	300	4	5	8	31
Yost Luckinbill	100	4	2	3	8
Sebastian Levan	280	4	4	8	30
Jost Ladig, shoemaker	--	1	1	--	1
Henry Lang	100	1	2	4	5
Peter Miller	--	1	1	--	1
Philip Mertz	--	--	1	--	1
John Mauser	--	2	2	--	2
John Minder	--	1	2	--	1
Nicho's Muffley, Sen'r	100	2	2	--	3
Peter Muffley, j'r	100	2	2	--	3
Conrad Metzger	100	3	2	3	7
Conrad Manesmith	150	6	4	4	18
Valentine Metzger	--	1	--	--	1
Jacob Meyer	--	--	1	--	1
Leonard Moyer	--	2	2	--	2
Fred'k Neindorf, taverner	100	2	6	--	8
Jacob Rein	--	1	--	--	1
Nicholas Quering	60	2	2	3	3
Philip Roadt	150	--	2	--	4
Jacob Scheffer	--	2	3	3	3
Michael Snyder	--	--	1	--	1
Joseph Sigfredt	300	4	3	5	25
Casper Smeck, sadler	150	2	2	--	4
Martin Seeh	--	1	--	--	1
Geo. Sell	150	4	3	4	15
Philip Scholl, g.m.	45	3	3	3	10
Jacob Sharadine	100	2	2	--	9
Jacob Hen. Sterner	252	4	2	4	9
Geo. Sheffer, b. smith	40	1	--	--	3
Andrew Sasseman	100	3	3	4	10
Henry Saseman	100	3	3	4	9
Geo. Saseman	100	3	2	4	10
Henry Sherrer	150	2	4	6	9
Peter Sherer	150	4	5	8	17
Nicholas Schwyer	150	4	4	6	9
John Sigfredt's, estate	300	4	3	6	19
Michael Shatz	--	--	1	--	1
Peter Smith, skinner	--	2	2	--	1
Henry Sweitzer	--	--	1	--	1
Christian Seibert	100	1	2	--	3
Chris. Fred. Steinbruh, b. smith	--	--	1	--	1
X'n Wanner	100	2	2	4	6
Jacob Weis	10	2	1	--	3
Deobald Winck	300	4	4	10	20
Michael Werrily	200	3	6	4	20

Maxatawny Township	Acres	Horses	Cattle	Sheep	Tax
John With	100	2	4	5	4
Henry Wetstone	150	5	4	4	12
Richard Wistar	500	--	--	--	40
John Weeser	--	--	1	--	1
Geo. Weymen	--	2	--	4	1
Joseph Wild	--	1	1	--	1
Geo. Zimmerman	100	3	2	5	6
Abram Zimerman	300	3	3	2	13
Bast'n Zimerman	350	5	6	9	34
George Weeser	--	--	1	--	1
Henry Grim	250	3	4	6	15
John Gross	--	1	1	--	2
William Gross	150	3	4	5	12
Joseph Gross	150	4	4	3	13

Single Men

	Shillings		Shillings
John Coller	15	Francis Stimel	15
Abram Wetstein	15	Christian Seibert	15
Mich'l Delong	15	John Muffle	15
Jacob Kutz	15	Henry Bast	15

Exeter Township

	Acres	Horses	Cattle	Sheep	Tax
Adam Allstadt, farmer	200	4	3	4	20
Henry Alder, mason	--	--	1	--	1
Adam Apple, labourer	--	--	1	--	1
David Bushberiger, blacksmith	--	--	--	--	1
James Boone, tanner	400	7	8	25	40
William Boone, farmer, g.m.	270	4	7	18	20
Joseph Boone, farmer	200	4	6	12	20
Jacob Boyer, farmer	100	2	3	4	18
John Boyer, blacksmith	--	2	1	--	1
Christ'r, & Son Boyer	170	3	2	6	15
Peter Bechtel	90	2	2	--	5
John Bechtel	150	3	2	--	14
Samuel Boone	160	2	2	9	15
Cha's Bingeman	--	--	--	--	1
Jacob Bechtel	225	4	3	2	19
John Bishop	100	3	2	6	13
Godfred Baker, carpenter	--	1	1	--	1
Geo. Beatam, miller	--	--	--	--	1
John Coch	100	1	1	--	2
Christ'n Coppleberger	100	2	3	--	4
Fredrick Christian	--	--	1	--	1
Mathias Deeter	150	3	4	--	17
Harman David, cordwainer	30	1	1	--	2
Paul Durst	290	4	5	10	22
Morris Ellis	130	3	4	12	14
John Ellis, shopkeeper	--	4	2	--	5

Exeter Township	Acres	Horses	Cattle	Sheep	Tax
Rowland Ellis	15	1	2	--	3
Fredrick Evil	--	--	--	--	1
Casper Egle	100	--	--	--	8
Elizabeth Esterly	200	2	3	--	6
John Failer, wheelwright	--	--	1	--	1
Caleb Feager	--	--	--	--	1
Fredrick Goodhart	150	2	4	8	12
Geo. Gerich	150	4	5	6	20
Godfrey Gring	150	2	2	--	5
Michael Hauck	--	1	1	--	2
Geo. Henton	150	4	4	6	12
Rob't Henton	70	2	1	--	2
Jacob Huet	100	2	2	5	6
Nicholas Harner	90	2	2	4	6
Ludwig Huet	100	2	1	--	4
Samuel Hughes	160	4	5	10	12
Edward Hughes	79	3	3	6	5
Geo. Hughes	150	3	4	--	12
Valentine Hartman	100	2	2	4	5
Rudolph, & Son Hegler	250	4	6	8	25
Geo. Heckman	--	--	--	--	1
Christian Huet	100	--	--	--	2
Fred'k Knochle	50	1	--	--	2
Joseph Kirby	100	2	2	--	8
Peter Kirby	100	--	--	--	8
W'm Kirby	100	3	2	--	13
Conrad Keller	--	--	1	--	1
Fred'k Kealler	--	1	1	--	1
Paul Kerber	17	1	1	--	2
Henry Knote	--	4	3	6	6
Jacob Lefler	200	2	1	--	12
Michael Ludwig	150	4	4	10	17
Mordecai Lincoln	200	2	2	--	10
Baltzer Leffler	100	2	2	--	5
Abraham Lincoln	320	3	3	10	19
Jacob Levan	150	4	6	4	20
Abraham Levan	300	4	5	4	17
Leonard Lebo	150	2	4	--	12
Conrad Merch	--	--	--	--	1
John Messersmith	250	3	3	--	8
Peter Null	100	2	2	6	1
Robert Patterson	50	2	2	--	2
Francis, & Son Rutter	300	4	5	7	24
Richard Penrose	180	2	3	6	6
W'm Patterson, weaver	--	--	--	--	1
George Rutter	150	4	5	--	15
Jacob Roun	350	3	3	8	14
George Sharer, blacksmith	--	--	--	--	1
Adam Scheirer	--	2	2	2	8
Peter Schnyder	230	3	5	9	16
John Stucker	--	1	2	--	1
Michael Seister	200	4	5	10	18
Geo. Snyder	60	--	1	--	2
Jacob Snyder	--	--	--	--	1
Abel Thomas	27	2	2	4	4

Exeter Township	Acres	Horses	Cattle	Sheep	Tax
James Thompson	10	2	2	4	4
Henry Thompson	85	2	3	10	6
John Thompson	100	2	2	5	4
Benjamin Tallman	100	2	2	5	4
William Tallman	--	1	1	--	2
Henry Vanderslice	40	3	2	--	8
James Webb, weaver	--	--	1	--	1
Christian Wicks	150	2	4	6	12
John, & Son Webb	180	3	4	--	10
Adam Wagoner	150	4	4	6	7
John Wainwright	100	--	1	--	2
Isaac Weisman	--	2	2	--	2
Martin Waltz	100	2	2	--	7
John Webb	--	--	--	--	1
Jacob Weiler	170	3	4	6	12
John Weidman	100	2	2	--	5
Adam Young	150	2	3	6	12
Valentine Young	30	1	1	--	2

Single Men

	Shillings		Shillings
Nathan Pugh	15	Israel Ritter	15
James Boone	15	Geo. Landers	15
Benjamin Boone	15	Christ'r Huyett	15
James Boone	15	Owen Williams	15
Dieter Bernhard	15	William Hopes	15
Lodowig Huet	15	Frederick Alder	15
John Dierling	15	Henry Boyer	15
Rob't Patterson	15	Adam Diem	15
Engle Boyer	15		

Windsor Township

	Acres	Horses	Cattle	Sheep	Tax
David Allspach	150	3	2	4	7
George Allspach	100	2	2	4	3
William Bossler	150	3	4	2	5
John Bock	100	--	2	4	2
William Berckheiser	100	1	2	--	2
Melchior Baun	100	--	--	--	2
Philip Bobemayer	100	1	1	--	2
John Breninger	100	2	2	3	4
Philip Bayer	50	1	1	--	2
Clementz Dunkelberger	100	2	3	3	5
Killian Dunkel	100	3	3	--	8
Michael Dewalt	200	2	2	4	7
Wendel Ernst	25	1	2	--	2
Peter Fogt	100	2	3	1	3
Conrad Finck	200	2	2	3	7
George Gordner	100	2	2	2	3
Evan Grean	194	8	2	3	6

31

Windsor Township	Acres	Horses	Cattle	Sheep	Tax
Henry Gross	80	2	2	4	3
Daniel Hill, Sen'r	100	2	2	--	2
Daniel Hill, Jun'r	200	2	3	--	6
Jacob Hill, Sen'r	100	2	2	2	4
Jacob Hill, Jun'r	200	3	4	4	8
Conrad Hausman	100	12	2	--	2
Wendel Hauer	100	2	3	4	6
Geo. Hauer	40	1	1	--	2
John Hauser	50	2	2	2	3
Michael Hollebach	50	1	1	--	2
Casper Hensel	50	2	2	--	9
Philip Hensel	50	2	2	--	3
John Heffer	100	2	2	--	2
Jacob Humel	50	2	2	4	4
Christian Hausknecht	100	2	3	3	6
Frederick Haass	150	2	2	--	5
Henry Hoff	30	1	1	--	2
Charles Heffle	--	--	--	--	2
Feit Hert	100	2	2	3	4
Philip Henckel	150	2	2	4	5
Geo. Heilman	50	2	1	--	2
Widow Hughes	100	2	2	--	2
Ulrick Hill	70	--	--	--	4
George Joe	200	4	4	9	10
Henry Kallbach	100	2	2	--	5
Adam Klein	100	2	2	3	4
Michael Kreicher	100	2	3	--	7
Bastian Kreisher	100	2	2	2	5
Conrad Kirschner	225	3	4	4	13
Daniel Kamb	70	2	2	--	2
Mathias Koch	150	2	1	--	2
Conrad Lora	150	2	2	--	4
Geo. Lindemuth	100	2	2	--	3
Adam Luckenbil	100	2	2	--	4
Jacob Loose	50	1	1	--	2
Geo. Merckel	50	1	2	2	3
Geo. Miller	250	2	3	6	11
George May	100	2	2	3	3
Andrew May	260	4	4	8	8
Jacob Miller	100	2	2	4	2
Henry Moll	300	2	3	--	8
Baltzer Neyfang	80	1	1	--	2
Geo. Pauch	80	2	1	--	2
Jacob Pettry	100	--	3	--	2
Leonhardt Rever	150	4	3	4	11
Geo. Rever	75	1	1	--	2
Jacob Rahn	100	--	--	--	2
Jacob Rausch	100	2	2	3	4
Martin Rausch	150	2	2	3	4
Joseph Rauner	100	1	1	--	2
Jeremiah Schappel	100	2	2	2	5
Thomas Starr	100	2	3	--	2
Eberhard Shappel	110	2	2	2	5
Henry Shumaker, s.m.	200	3	4	--	6
Casper Schmit	50	--	1	--	2

Windsor Township

	Acres	Horses	Cattle	Sheep	Tax
John Sheffer	100	1	2	--	2
Michael Shleir	100	2	2	--	3
Peter Stirstler	100	2	2	--	3
Geo. Stenger	100	2	2	--	2
Geo. Schnyder	120	2	2	3	4
Henry Scheurer	100	2	2	--	4
Godfred Seidel	200	2	2	4	8
Andrew Seidel	100	2	2	--	4
Michael Unger	100	2	2	--	4
Nicho's Weininger	150	2	1	--	5
Nicho's Wengert	100	2	2	--	4
Gerhart Will	150	2	2	--	5
Peter Weber	150	2	1	2	2
Thomas Wright	100	4	4	8	6
Bernhardt Zweitzig	100	2	1	1	3
Abram Luckinbill	--	--	--	--	2
Geo. Klein	--	--	--	--	2
And'w Dielman	--	--	--	--	2
Martin Humel	--	--	--	--	1
Andrew Humel	--	--	--	--	1
John Blattner	--	--	--	--	1
Conrad Blattner	--	--	--	--	1
Adam Schwenkert	--	--	--	--	1
Nicholas Riehm	--	--	--	--	1
Daniel Joh	--	--	--	--	1
Geo. Lantzer	--	--	--	--	1
Stephen Hars	--	--	--	--	1
Conrad Hartinger	--	--	--	--	1

Single Men

	Shillings		Shillings
Adam Rever	15	Charles McClasky	15
Michael Beck	15	John Hughes	15
Clementz Dunkelberg	15	Evan Hughes	15
Martin Neufang	15	Philip Allspach	15
Charles Shoemaker	15	Fredrick Paust	15

Heidelberg Township

	Acres	Horses	Cattle	Sheep	Tax
John Arbengast	25	--	1	--	2
John Artz	100	4	6	6	21
William Allen, Esq'r	500	--	--	--	60
Adam Ares, taylor	--	1	1	--	2
Simon Aigler, shoemaker	30	1	2	--	2
Peter Alman, skinner	--	--	--	--	2
John Boyer, Sen'r	200	4	4	4	24
Henry Baurer	140	4	2	3	4
John Boyer, Jun'r	100	3	2	2	10
Henry Brintz	30	2	2	--	2
George Brendle	100	4	3	4	6

33

Heidelberg Township	Acres	Horses	Cattle	Sheep	Tax
Tobias Breckel	150	3	3	4	7
Samuel Boyer	80	2	2	4	6
Andreas Boyer	200	4	4	4	23
John Bricker	70	4	4	4	11
Adam Braun	100	3	3	4	10
Frantz Brossman, turner	150	1	--	--	6
John Brossman	--	2	1	--	3
Geo. Braun	100	4	3	6	10
Casper Breninger	--	--	--	--	1
Assimus Beyer	60	2	2	--	2
Christopher Bickley, turner	50	2	2	--	2
Ulrick Bruner	50	--	2	1	3
Philip Bahm	--	--	--	--	1
Michael Busch	100	2	2	--	3
Philip Baur	--	1	1	--	1
Bernhard Bob	--	2	1	--	4
John Blank	100	2	2	--	6
Peter Boyer	80	1	1	--	2
Michael Berger	--	--	--	--	1
Nicholas Bechtel	--	2	1	--	2
Henry Deckert	100	2	2	3	4
Philip Deshler	50	1	1	--	4
John Dieter	190	2	2	2	9
Christian Deppy	300	3	3	3	17
William Davis	--	2	1	--	4
Bastian Erich	30	2	2	--	3
Peter Eberley	100	2	2	2	15
Martin Ernoldt	50	2	2	--	3
Eleazor Evans	200	3	3	5	17
Christ'n Eberhard	50	--	--	1	2
John Ekert, taylor	180	5	4	--	22
Conrad Eckert	100	4	2	--	10
Conrad Ernst	100	2	2	--	8
Jacob Erb	100	2	2	--	2
John Feg	100	1	1	--	6
Wm. Fisher	100	4	4	4	16
Philip Fisher	50	1	1	--	2
John Fisher	50	1	1	--	2
Peter Fetzer	--	--	--	--	1
Henry Fidler	200	2	2	--	18
Ludwig Fisher	100	2	2	2	13
Peter Fisher	100	1	3	3	10
Adam Fucks	50	2	2	3	4
Michael Faust	--	--	--	--	1
Peter Feg	100	2	2	2	6
Stephen Fidler	--	--	--	--	1
Jost Filsmeyer	200	3	3	--	19
Anthony Faust	100	2	4	3	17
Christian Frantz	100	2	2	--	3
Andreas Fassler, weaver	--	--	--	--	1
Jost Fishbach, wagoner	50	1	1	--	2
Michael Foltz	40	--	2	1	2
Peter Faust	100	1	1	--	2
Christ'n Frymier	100	2	2	3	11
John Frantz	--	1	1	--	1

Heidelberg Township

	Acres	Horses	Cattle	Sheep	Tax
Henry Fisher	50	1	1	--	2
Henry Gruber	200	3	3	3	15
Adam Gruber	--	2	2	--	2
Geo. Gensmer, skiner	--	--	--	--	2
Nicholas Glatt	100	2	2	2	3
Jacob Greeder	--	2	3	6	2
Fred'k Gerhart	200	2	2	2	8
Casper Gabel	25	--	1	1	1
Henry Gebbard	--	--	--	--	1
Michael Grau, 2 g. & s.m.'s	100	2	2	3	9
Alexander Grau	100	2	2	3	7
Nicholas Glotz, b'smith	--	--	--	--	1
George Herold	150	3	3	2	10
George Haine	150	3	3	--	15
Frederick Haine, 2 g. & s.m.'s	280	4	4	--	20
Peter Haus	150	2	3	--	7
Christian Hain	50	2	1	--	22
Ludwig Held	200	4	4	4	20
John Heckert, sadler	--	1	2	2	4
Adam Hain	300	2	4	2	27
Henry Hain	200	4	2	--	15
Bastian Hossler	50	--	2	2	2
Henry Hushar	25	--	1	1	2
John Hofferdt	--	--	--	--	1
Michael Hoell	50	1	2	2	4
John Hain, 2 s. & g.m.'s	200	--	--	--	13
Henry Hetterich	--	--	--	--	1
Jacob Hochstatler	40	1	1	--	1
Jacob Joder	100	2	2	--	4
George Jockle	--	1	2	3	1
Thomas Jones, Jr.	100	2	2	2	4
Thomas Jones	200	4	6	6	16
Jacob Jagley	50	--	1	--	2
Frederick Kobel, 2 g. & s.m.'s	200	2	2	2	26
John Koble	100	2	2	--	11
Melchior Kuhn	--	--	--	--	1
George Kab	100	1	1	1	1
John Koehler	100	2	2	--	4
Francis Krick	50	--	--	--	3
Henry Klein	--	--	--	--	1
Frederick Klamer	--	--	--	--	1
John Keller	80	2	2	--	5
Peter Knob	100	2	2	3	9
Peter Kuhl	90	2	2	3	6
Peter Klob	100	3	2	5	8
Abraham Kesler	60	1	1	1	2
Christian Kelbach	30	1	1	--	2
Fred'k Klassbrener, taylor	50	--	1	--	3
Michael Kesler	100	--	2	2	2
Jacob Kuhl	150	4	4	4	8
John Klinger	100	2	3	4	3
Henry Knob	60	1	1	2	3
Frederick Kohr	--	1	1	--	1
Geo. Lang, shoemaker	100	--	--	--	2
Martin Long, shoemaker	60	2	1	--	2

Heidelberg Township	Acres	Horses	Cattle	Sheep	Tax
Paul Lebo	--	1	1	--	2
Mich'l Laur, Jr.	--	--	--	--	1
Michael Laur	100	2	2	--	7
Peter Laman	100	2	2	--	3
Christ'r Lerck	100	2	2	2	4
Anthony Lambrecht, b'smith	70	2	1	--	4
Daniel Ludwig, g.m.	100	4	4	8	12
Godlieb Leffeler	--	--	--	--	1
Geo. Louck	200	--	--	--	2
George Laug	200	5	4	6	20
Jacob Leininger	50	1	1	2	2
Martin Linck, 2 g. & s.m.'s	30	1	2	--	3
John Lesch	100	2	2	2	4
Thomas Lenich	60	2	2	--	2
Paul Lingel	150	4	4	5	9
Mathias Miller, weaver	25	--	1	--	1
John Meth	200	3	2	4	12
Geo. Mauntz	100	2	2	--	5
Joseph Mauntz	100	2	2	--	5
Lorentz Mourer	--	--	--	--	1
John Meyer	200	2	3	--	10
Jacob Moore	30	2	1	2	2
Dietrich Marshall	200	4	8	6	27
Ulrich Michael	100	4	2	2	5
Michael Miller	100	2	2	2	6
Peter Numan	60	2	1	--	3
Christopher Naugle	100	2	2	--	2
George Neu	--	--	--	--	1
Michael Overheiser	30	1	1	--	2
Jacob Oxenreider	40	--	1	--	1
John Patton	1,000	16	3	--	40
Martin Patteiger	100	2	2	--	7
John Palm	50	1	1	2	2
Casper Reed	--	2	2	--	2
George Rab	--	--	--	--	1
John Reidenbach	100	2	2	2	4
Peter Ruth	100	--	--	--	10
John Roescher	150	2	2	--	15
Peter Reedy	100	2	2	--	6
Ulrich Ritchard	100	2	2	--	6
John Reaber	100	2	2	--	6
Jacob Rehrer	--	1	1	--	4
George Rau	--	--	--	--	1
John Rau	25	1	1	--	2
Andreas Rab, smith	--	--	--	--	1
Weirich Seltzer	59	1	1	--	3
Peter Schuy	125	3	2	2	13
Michael Schaffer	--	--	--	--	1
Joacam Smith	--	--	--	--	1
Nicholas Saladine, butcher	--	--	--	--	1
Jacob Seltzer	25	1	1	--	6
Michael Smeal	165	1	4	6	17
Philip Spohn	150	4	4	3	15
John Scheffer	50	2	2	--	2
Henry Stear	150	2	2	2	6

Heidelberg Township	Acres	Horses	Cattle	Sheep	Tax
John Steiner	100	2	4	6	5
Michael Snyder	60	2	2	--	2
Benjamin Weiser	200	--	2	2	4
Leibright Wagoner, taylor	--	--	--	--	1
Lazarus Wingard	160	4	4	--	8
Peter Werlau	--	--	--	--	1
Fredrick Weiser, 2 g. & s.m.'s	300	4	5	3	20
Peter Werner	148	2	2	--	4
Geo. Worheim	--	1	--	--	1
Baltzer Wenrick	50	2	2	4	3
Thomas Wenrich	--	--	--	--	1
Mathias Wenrich, Sen'r	100	2	2	4	8
Mathias Wenrich, Jr.	50	2	2	2	3
Philip Wagoner	25	1	2	--	2
John Walsmith	100	2	2	4	6
Henry Worheim	--	--	--	--	1
John Wenrich, smith	100	2	2	6	8
Philip Wobensmith	25	1	1	--	2
Dieter Wurtz	--	--	--	--	1
John Zerbe, g.r.	140	4	4	7	8
Henry Spath	50	2	3	6	6
Casper Sheeffer	100	2	1	--	3
Lorentz Struck	100	2	2	3	5
Dietrich Sohl	--	--	--	--	2
Yost Sugar	100	2	1	--	4
Henry Sugar	100	4	4	5	16
Eliz'a Shaurin, wid'o	100	2	2	--	5
Jacob Smith	80	2	2	--	2
Peter Sensebach	100	2	2	--	17
Christian Schlectig	36	2	2	--	2
Dietrich Steinbrecher	--	--	--	--	1
Nicholas Scheffer	100	2	2	2	8
Peter Stroul	--	--	--	--	1
Conrad Scharff	150	2	3	4	7
Rudolph Smeltzer	--	--	--	--	1
Peter Sohl	100	1	1	--	5
Peter Schonfelder	--	1	1	--	1
Henry Sohl	--	--	--	--	1
Jacob Strunck	--	--	--	--	1
Dieter Stella	--	--	--	--	1

Single Men

	Shillings		Shillings
John Haine	15	Jacob Feg	15
Fred'k Haine	15	Nicholas Lingel	15
Nicho's Bob	15	John Blanck	15
Philip Hecker	15	Henry Schuker	15
Michael Fisher	15	John Kuhl	15
Philip Werheim	15	Geo. Brendel	15
Geo. Leininger	15	Fred'k Gerhard	15
John Lindenman	15	Henry Bauer	15
John Grotheiser	15	Conrad Christ	15
Geo. Kapp	15	Jacob Lorch	15

	Shillings		Shillings
Valentine Wolf	15	Henry Lauer	15
John Wingert	15	James Davids	15
Benj'a Weiser	15		

Single Men

Eastern District Township

	Acres	Horses	Cattle	Sheep	Tax
Frederick Batz	25	1	1	--	2
Jacob Busch	50	1	1	--	3
Jeremiah Bacon	25	2	1	2	3
Martin Borkhard	--	--	--	--	1
Samuel Banfield	100	2	2	--	7
Conrad Christian, weaver	10	1	1	--	2
Mathias Dotterer	30	--	1	--	2
Henry Denier, shoemaker	25	1	1	--	2
Fredrick Fredrick	50	--	1	--	2
Peter Gutman, taylor	--	--	--	--	1
Jacob Harb	50	1	2	--	2
Geo. Hartlein	150	3	6	4	8
Michael Hofman	25	1	1	--	2
Michael Hartman	10	1	1	--	2
Fredrick Hoof, wheelright	--	--	1	--	3
Adam Heeter	--	1	1	--	1
Geo. Holtzchoe	20	1	1	--	2
Adam Imbody	70	2	2	3	4
Philip Yaxthaimer	--	--	--	--	1
Nicholas Koontz	50	2	2	--	9
Conrad Keim	100	2	2	--	9
Joseph Lahman	100	2	2	--	4
Christian Lookenbill	25	1	1	--	1
Jacob Lorentz	10	1	1	--	1
John Miller	100	2	3	3	8
Frantz Mosser	100	3	2	4	5
William Miller, butcher	10	--	1	--	1
Dietrich Martin	150	3	2	3	14
Fredrick Mayer	100	2	3	3	8
John Oyster	100	2	3	8	15
Geo. Oyster	50	2	2	3	7
Samuel Oyster, b'smith	25	--	1	--	5
John Reitenaur	100	2	1	--	5
Jacob Rood	100	2	3	4	8
Martin Rehr, shoemaker	--	--	--	--	1
Jacob Seiberd	25	--	1	--	1
Michael Stauch	40	--	1	--	3
John Schot, mason	25	1	--	--	1
William Stork	50	2	1	--	4
Jacob Steinbrener	30	1	1	2	2
Valentine Schaffer	--	--	--	--	--
Jacob Schmidt	25	--	1	--	1
Anthony Smit	40	--	--	1	2
Leonhard Scheffer	20	--	1	--	1
Samuel Spaht, mason	--	--	--	--	2
Peter Weller	100	2	3	3	12

Eastern District Township	Acres	Horses	Cattle	Sheep	Tax
Paul Weyand	25	1	1	--	2
Reinard Weis	--	--	--	--	1
Gottleib Weidaw	--	--	--	--	1
Carl Weis	25	1	2	--	2
Jacob Walter	--	--	--	--	1
Lazarus Weidner	20	--	--	--	1
Wm. Mayburry	500	--	--	--	15
Thomas Rutter, Ex'r	150	--	--	--	7
Stephen Reppert	--	--	--	--	8
Sabina Hess	--	--	--	--	8
Michael Long	--	--	--	--	7
Peter Keplinger	--	--	--	--	5
Valentine Dillinger	--	--	--	--	3
Jacob Hamm	--	--	--	--	3
Henry Makenet	--	--	--	--	1
Abraham Bechtle	--	--	--	--	5
Peter Bechtle	--	--	--	--	5
Peter Trautman	--	--	--	--	6
Andreas Seibert	--	--	--	--	1
Adolph Mayer	--	--	--	--	2
Andreas Grad	--	--	--	--	2
Melchior Raberd	--	--	--	--	2

Single Men

	Shillings		Shillings
Balthazar Bohm	15	Henry Imbody	15
Daniel Oyster	15	Peter Martin	15
John Coltren	15	Conrad Schleiger	15

Western District Township

	Acres	Horses	Cattle	Sheep	Tax
John Barntz, mason	100	2	2	--	2
John Borsch	--	--	1	--	1
Charles Maburry, forgeman	--	--	--	--	1
Mathias Coober, weaver	--	--	1	--	1
Michael Dotterer	50	1	1	--	2
Geo. Dotterer	100	3	3	--	8
Joshua Delaplain	100	2	2	2	4
Leon'd Drumheller	--	1	1	--	1
Cornelius Dehart	50	--	--	--	2
Mary Margaret Dolingerin	25	--	--	--	1
Daniel East, b'smith	100	2	2	4	6
Jacob Eberhard	20	1	1	--	1
Nicho's Elenschleger	--	--	1	--	1
Fredrick Eberle	--	--	1	--	1
Casper Griesemer	25	--	--	--	1
Geo. Grisle	--	--	1	--	1
Jacob Gelbach	50	--	--	--	3
Geo. Glawser, mason	80	2	2	--	5

Western District Township	Acres	Horses	Cattle	Sheep	Tax
Sam'l Gay	50	--	--	--	3
Stephen Hawk	100	2	2	4	8
Jacob Hill	200	4	6	8	26
Philip Hardman, weaver	--	--	1	--	1
George Hardman	25	--	--	--	1
Richards James	--	--	1	--	4
John Yager	25	--	--	--	1
Peter Yoder	--	--	--	--	4
Martin Klotz, weaver	70	1	1	--	2
Jacob Klotz	100	2	2	2	4
Jost Maninger	50	2	2	3	2
John Motzer, sadler	100	1	2	6	7
Philip Mathias	120	2	2	4	8
Dietrich Matha, taylor	40	1	1	--	4
John Old, & Co., f.	500	4	1	--	50
Edward Optegraft	10	--	1	--	1
Henry Reemer	100	2	1	--	3
Henry Reeath	40	--	--	--	2
Conrad Rooth	90	--	--	--	3
Adam Schwabel	--	--	1	--	1
Lorentz Sheeler, f.m.	25	1	1	--	3
Geo. Steibensand	50	1	1	1	4
William Stapleton	25	--	--	--	1
Geo. Schall, wheelright	150	3	3	5	10
Geo. Weidner, Ad.	200	4	5	6	22
Geo. Weitner, Jr., Ad.	--	--	1	--	1
Jacob Weaver	50	--	--	--	2
John Potts	100	--	--	--	5

Single Men

	Shillings			Shillings
Peter Keim	15		Joshua Delaplain	15

Greenwich Township

	Acres	Horses	Cattle	Sheep	Tax
Martin Ably, weaver	25	--	1	--	2
George Bauman	100	2	2	--	4
Thomas Baltzer	30	2	2	--	2
Andrew Bollick	--	--	--	--	1
Lorentz Beiber	200	2	2	2	6
Adam Bowr	30	2	1	--	3
Conrad Bower	100	2	2	1	3
Henry Berck	100	1	1	--	3
Ludwig Berckel	--	--	--	--	1
Henry Bollender	120	2	2	--	3
Peter Beely	50	2	1	1	4
Leonard Bowman	80	2	2	2	4
Martin Biglar	60	2	1	--	2
Conrad Baver	100	2	2	4	5
Jacob Bower	--	--	1	--	1

Greenwich Township	Acres	Horses	Cattle	Sheep	Tax
Jacob Back	--	--	--	--	1
Charles Balmer	100	2	2	2	2
Rudolph Bosserd	150	3	2	--	6
Henry Chrisman	130	--	--	--	6
Philip Clonninger	120	2	2	--	2
Nicholas Baron	60	--		--	2
Adam Dell	100	2	2	2	4
Peter Dunckel	250	4	4	4	11
Simon Durck	--	1	--	--	1
John Durck	--	--	--	--	1
Simon Eisenberger	60	2	1	--	1
Nicholas Eisenman	50	--	1	--	1
John Fuss	140	4	3	3	5
Adam Faust	100	2	2	--	4
Jacob Faust	130	1	1	2	4
Henry Faust	150	3	3	3	7
Nicholas Gotschall	100	2	2	2	5
Fredrick Greamer	250	4	5	5	12
Geo. Greamer	200	3	3	5	10
Godfred Greamer	100	3	2	4	8
Geo. Gearling	--	--	--	--	1
Abraham Glas	40	--	--	--	--
Geo. Hollabach	60	1	--	--	2
Geo. Hildebrand, f.m., s.m.	100	2	2	2	5
John Humel, b. smith	--	--	--	--	1
Henry Hava	80	1	1	--	2
Fredrick Humel	50	2	1	--	2
Peter Hatinger, b. smith	--	--	--	--	1
Fredrick Haman	100	2	2	--	5
Peter Hall, shoemaker	45	1	1	--	2
John Horring	80	2	2	--	5
Geo. Horring, wheelright	90	2	2	--	5
Ludwig Haspelhorn, mason	80	1	2	--	2
John Deel Herman	140	2	2	2	4
Adam Kalbach	100	2	2	--	3
Geo. Krubach	--	--	--	--	3
Mathias Keffer	100	2	2	2	6
John Kus	100	2	2	--	4
Geo. Kamp	150	2	2	--	6
George Kosser	250	4	3	4	10
Geo. Kosser, j'r	--	--	--	--	1
Martin Keffer	100	2	2	2	5
John Koller	100	2	2	2	5
Andorius Kiehl	100	2	3	2	5
Geo. Keller	--	--	--	--	1
William Jans	50	--	1	--	2
Geo. Ley	150	2	2	4	5
Michael Ley	100	2	2	4	3
Fredrick Leiby	100	3	3	3	6
Jacob Leiby	150	3	3	3	8
George Mich'l Leiby	140	2	3	2	6
Nicho's Hollebach	--	--	--	--	1
Nicholas Linn	100	2	2	2	3
Jacob Latig, b. smith	100	2	2	3	3
Jacob Leonard	125	2	3	2	4

41

Greenwich Township	Acres	Horses	Cattle	Sheep	Tax
Philip Leonard, wheelwright	100	2	3	--	4
Michael Lescher	100	3	3	4	10
Michael Laub	25	--	1	--	4
John Lang	30	--	--	--	1
Bernhard Minig	--	--	--	--	1
Fred'k Mauser	50	1	2	1	2
Henry Minich	50	--	--	--	1
Philip Mayer	25	2	1	--	2
Geo. Markel, schoolmast'r	--	--	2	--	1
Henry Mayer	67	1	1	--	2
Jacob Mack	25	--	1	--	1
George Adam Mayer	100	2	1	2	3
Fred'k Mayer	200	4	4	4	11
Geo. Miller	100	2	2	2	1
Mich'l Miller, b. smith	--	--	--	--	1
Philip Miller	--	1	2	--	1
Dan'l Manesmith	--	--	--	--	1
Elias Rethga	70	2	1	--	2
Conrad Rigelman	100	1	1	2	1
Mathias Remer	100	3	2	1	6
Christ'r Rein	--	--	--	--	1
John Rousch	--	--	--	--	1
Geo. Spoon	100	1	2	2	4
Geo. Spang	50	1	1	--	1
Adam Smith	--	--	--	--	1
Henry Smith	50	--	--	--	1
Peter Smith	80	2	2	--	2
Nicho's Schomaker	150	4	3	4	7
X'r Schlenker	100	--	1	--	2
Fredrick Schlenker	100	1	1	--	3
John Schuck	--	--	--	--	1
Henry Sollenberger	50	1	1	--	2
Adam Smith	--	--	--	--	1
Michael Smith, shoemaker	50	1	2	--	2
Lorence Schollenberger	150	4	4	3	9
Gerhard Schollenberger	80	2	2	1	4
Joseph Schnep	--	--	--	--	1
Geo. Schwenck	--	--	--	--	1
John Sasemanhausen	150	3	3	5	8
Peter Steirwald	100	2	3	--	4
Godfred Stearn	28	1	2	--	2
Andrew Treslar, b. smith	130	3	3	4	7
W'm Trautman	70	--	2	--	2
Martin Unangst	25	2	--	--	2
Christian Ungerer	100	1	2	2	2
Jacob Wiltraud, weaver	100	1	1	--	3
Anthony Walter	150	2	2	2	7
Jacob Wery	100	2	2	--	3
Craft Weaver	70	2	2	--	3
Geo. Weyman	100	--	--	--	2
Jacob Zettlemayer	60	3	2	--	3
Rudolph Zimer	100	2	3	3	6

Single Men

	Shillings		Shillings
Geo. Kremer	15	Sebastian Faust	15
Abraham Fry	15	Stophel Kramer	15
Henry Balmer	15		

Union Township

	Acres	Horses	Cattle	Sheep	Tax
Mark Bird, ironmaster, s.m., g.m., f.m.	1,000	14	10	30	105
Robert Bell	--	1	1	--	1
James Burn	--	--	1	--	1
John Bittler	300	3	6	--	15
Davey Davis	--	--	1	--	1
Geo. Douglas	100	--	--	--	3
Edw'd Dehaven	14	3	2	5	10
Patrick Collins, weaver	--	--	--	--	1
Evan Evans	150	2	3	8	8
Henry France	50	2	2	--	6
Peter Flicker	--	--	1	--	1
John Godfrey	100	2	3	10	15
Mordecai Harris	100	2	2	--	8
Edward Hughes	60	2	2	--	8
Owen Hughes	100	2	2	--	8
Israel Hughes	101	2	2	--	6
John Harrison	300	3	4	12	18
Andrew Hofman	84	1	1	--	2
Peter Haas, wheelwright	70	2	3	--	8
John Haas	50	1	2	--	3
James Ingels	43	--	--	--	3
Mounce Jones	200	2	4	10	10
Geo. Kerston	250	4	4	10	24
John Kerlin	50	--	--	--	2
Geo. Koutz	--	--	2	--	1
John Kampbell	--	1	--	--	2
Morgan Lewis	200	2	2	4	4
John Leopold	--	1	1	--	1
Thomas Lloyd	200	--	--	--	12
Lardner Lynford, & Co.	1,000	--	--	--	50
Joseph Millard	130	2	4	--	12
Mordecai Millard, farmer, g.m., s.m.	180	2	4	12	14
Jane Millard	100	2	3	4	5
Derick Penebecker	230	4	2	7	16
Jonathan Millard	47	1	1	--	--
Owen Richard	--	1	--	--	1
James Roberts	100	2	2	--	9
Owen Reinhard	100	2	3	10	12
Jacob Redche	100	2	2	--	11
Jacob Switzer, joiner	100	3	4	5	12
John Stoner	400	4	8	7	22
Conrad Snyder	--	1	2	--	2
Ludwig Strouble	--	--	2	--	1
Andreas Spiceline	--	--	2	--	1
Ludwig Schaeffer	--	1	1	--	1
Christian Schaffer	--	--	1	--	1

Union Township	Acres	Horses	Cattle	Sheep	Tax
Andrew Smith	--	--	1	--	1
John Umsted	170	4	3	6	18
John Vanhorne	25	2	2	3	2
Abram Whisler	100	2	3	--	9
John Wanger, farmer	277	3	4	4	18
Philip Wert	150	2	4	8	10
Abram Wanger, farmer	150	3	5	10	20
Isaac Weisman	--	--	1	--	1
Daniel Yoder	200	3	3	6	7

Single Men

	Shillings		Shillings
Joseph Millard	15	John Tickle	15
Jacob Howard	15	Sam'l Philips	15
Sam'l Cox	15	Fredrick Warlick	15
Martin Wert	15		

Douglas Township

	Acres	Horses	Cattle	Sheep	Tax
Reinholdt Auvenshine	60	2	2	3	3
George Dieter Bucker, g.m.	150	1	3	6	14
Stophel Biddle	50	2	2	2	5
Nicholas Bunn	50	3	2	--	7
John Close	--	1	--	--	1
Derick Cleaver	--	1	--	--	3
Geo. Christ, s.m.	40	1	2	--	8
Jacob Davenheiser	70	2	3	4	5
Thomas Dealeth	50	1	1	--	2
Henry Eagle	150	2	3	3	9
Marcus Huling	100	2	2	4	9
Geo. Honselman	50	2	2	--	5
Michael Hofman	200	4	3	--	13
John Hofeman, weaver	--	--	1	--	1
Nicho's Handwark	100	2	2	5	12
Jacob Isenhower, carpenter	7	--	1	--	1
Valentine Keely, g.m.	350	4	5	9	30
Peter Levegood	72	2	3	--	6
Jacob Levegood	200	2	5	--	10
Thomas May	100	12	6	26	65
Peter Mefferd	150	3	3	4	15
John Mauger	200	2	3	5	13
Thomas Mayberry, forgeman	--	1	--	--	2
Martin Miller	150	4	4	--	12
Peter Mack, forgeman	--	--	--	--	1
Yoacam Naugle	150	2	4	8	17
Peter Niman	18	1	1	--	2
Comp'y Poole	200	--	--	--	10
John Romich	10	3	3	--	10
Michael Rafesnyder	30	--	--	--	2

Douglas Township	Acres	Horses	Cattle	Sheep	Tax
John Sarch	--	1	--	--	1
Peter Saler, forgeman	--	1	--	--	2
Geo. Shelter	270	3	4	--	11
Michael Spotz	35	2	2	1	8
Peter Shaner	100	2	2	--	8
Simon Smith	7	--	1	--	2
William Snider, fidler	10	1	1	--	2
Geo. Shock	--	--	--	--	1
Conrad Smith	7	--	1	--	2
John Swinehard	100	2	2	2	7
Baltas Simon, joiner	7	--	1	--	1
Henry Vanreed	200	--	--	--	8
Charles Witz, lock maker	150	4	4	6	14
Baltzer Wentzel	7	1	1	--	1
Peter Yocam	150	4	5	12	16
Jonas Yocam	150	2	2	1	12

Single Men

	Shillings			Shillings
John Derr	15		Thomas Harbird	15
John Keeley	15		John Betts	15

Hereford Township

	Acres	Horses	Cattle	Sheep	Tax
Geo. Akker	250	4	4	--	7
Widow Adams	60	1	1	--	2
Michael Bauer	192	3	4	4	13
Samuel Bauer	159	2	4	7	8
John Bechtel	150	2	6	4	11
Abraham Bechtel, weaver	115	2	4	7	9
Maria Bechtel	130	2	4	6	7
Abram Bauman	150	3	4	--	8
Geo. Beyer, weaver	100	2	4	4	7
Theobald Beck	100	2	1	--	2
Philip Beck	--	--	--	--	2
Philip Basdres	35	--	2	--	2
Henry Bortz	200	2	2	5	10
Peter Deisher	10	1	2	--	2
Joseph Erman	250	4	4	5	14
Christian Eschback	150	3	5	--	10
Peter Federolf	300	6	6	7	23
Peter Federolf	--	--	1	--	2
Nicholas Finck	130	3	4	5	7
Peter Fisher	150	3	3	--	14
Jacob Fisher	12	1	2	3	2
John Fisher	120	--	--	--	6
Philip Gerry	20	--	1	--	2
Len'd Greesmer	199	4	6	12	16
Jacob Greesemer	36	1	2	--	3

45

Hereford Township	Acres	Horses	Cattle	Sheep	Tax
Ludwig Gauker	200	4	4	5	8
Christian Geaman	200	3	5	5	7
Hanes Geaman, wagoner	90	2	1	--	4
John Gregory	200	3	3	4	14
Andreas Gregory	150	2	3	2	6
John Greett, taverner	50	2	4	--	4
Casper Hoffman	10	1	1	--	1
Freter Henrich	--	--	1	--	1
Christ'n Hoffman, weaver	80	1	2	--	2
Abra'm Herb, shoemaker	60	2	2	4	2
Jacob Han	--	--	--	--	--
Jacob Latscher	190	2	4	7	10
Henry Gibson, b. smith	--	--	--	--	1
Daniel Kreder	200	4	4	3	10
Peter Kunkel	175	4	4	6	14
John Kunius, joiner	36	2	2	--	5
Martin Kleber, shopkeeper	8	2	2	--	2
Ulrich Kuly	50	2	2	3	4
Adam Kerchner	200	4	3	4	10
Philip Lahr	125	2	4	2	9
Geo. Lahr	125	2	3	6	10
Frantz Latscher	130	3	1	--	11
Abraham Latscher	150	3	5	7	4
Benedick Lieser	150	2	4	3	10
Mich'l Leeser	150	2	3	3	4
Sam'l Lieser	200	2	3	4	5
Jacob Liebeguth	25	1	1	--	2
Conrad Ludwig	80	3	3	2	9
Tho's Mayburry	1,000	1	--	--	40
Geo. Masteller, b. smith	90	2	2	2	4
Tho's Mayburry	--	--	--	--	10
David Meschter, shoemaker	100	3	4	--	8
Christophel Mester	150	2	8	6	7
Eliz. Meyer	50	1	3	--	8
Jacob Miller	200	4	5	6	13
Fredrick Nester	60	2	3	--	2
Jacob Reyber	--	1	2	--	1
William Richard	150	2	2	3	5
Killian Rus	50	2	2	--	6
George Rohrbach	150	2	1	--	3
John Ritter	400	5	7	17	20
Fredrick Seyler	--	--	--	--	1
Conrad Schaub	35	--	--	--	2
Peter Sell	150	2	3	5	6
Michael Schell	100	3	4	6	3
Martin Stertzman	40	2	2	--	2
Peter Stroch	--	--	2	--	1
Hans Steman	160	3	2	--	7
Geo. Steman	160	2	3	--	11
Benedict Strohm	30	1	2	--	1
Hanes Staufer	169	2	3	--	12
Casper Strom	--	--	1	--	1
And's Sigfred	--	--	2	--	1
Melchior Schultz	250	4	7	11	20
Christ'r Schultz	170	4	6	6	12

Hereford Township

	Acres	Horses	Cattle	Sheep	Tax
X'n Schumaker	--	--	1	--	1
W'm Spera, taylor	65	--	--	--	1
Geo. Wugner	296	4	9	7	23
Valent Weybel	15	2	3	4	5
Jacob Witmer	--	--	1	--	2
Jacob Wetzel	110	3	3	4	4
Barba Geakkle	120	4	4	6	8
Balt'r Zimmerman	280	2	3	--	6
George Zerr, taylor	100	2	2	2	4
John Yeakle	50	--	--	--	2
Geo. Schultz	50	--	--	--	2
Michael Moll	50	--	--	--	2
John Mock	70	--	--	--	3

Single Men

	Shillings		Shillings
John Bower	15	John Retter	15
John Gearhard	15	Valentine Hould	15
David Gretter	15	John Sweinman	15
Jacob Fedderolf	15	Gerhard Bechtel	15
Peter Gearhard	15	Jacob Bechtel	15

Amity Township

	Acres	Horses	Cattle	Sheep	Tax
Daniel Andrew	150	4	4	6	10
Abraham Andrew	83	3	4	6	4
Abraham Brosius, inn keeper	100	4	2	25	11
Hugh Boone	347	4	8	12	30
Isaac Boone	200	2	3	3	11
John Boyer	200	3	4	10	14
Nicholas Boyer	150	4	4	8	17
George Bower	--	1	1	4	2
Moses Bower	--	2	2	--	1
Jacob Bower	200	2	3	12	11
Solomon Bromfield, shopkeeper	45	2	3	12	11
Joseph Bromfield	150	3	3	10	10
Henry Brosius, taylor	--	--	1	--	1
Martin Begher, inn keeper	155	4	3	--	19
Alex'r Bryan	--	--	1	--	1
Jacob Cline, blacksmith	35	1	2	5	4
Jeremiah Cefferly, blacksmith	150	2	3	6	8
John Carling, blacksmith	150	3	3	6	23
Philip Cole, inn keeper	--	3	1	6	4
John Child, hatter	--	1	--	--	1
Robt. Cambpel, schoolmaster	--	1	--	--	1
Frans. Carling	100	2	3	5	1
Baltzer Coppus	--	--	2	--	1
Nicholas Cydle	190	--	--	--	10
Corn's Dehart	130	3	4	11	15

47

Amity Township	Acres	Horses	Cattle	Sheep	Tax
Wm. Davis	--	1	--	--	1
Geo. Douglas, Esq'r, shopkeeper	175	1	--	--	30
David Davis	220	3	4	12	11
Dav'd Davis, doct'r	--	3	2	--	1
Jacob Diveler	40	1	2	--	6
Samuel Dehart	200	1	2	4	8
Daniel Fraley	4	--	--	--	1
Geo. Foos	280	3	4	6	22
Geo. Fritz	200	--	1	--	2
John Fritz, blacksmith	200	4	5	10	13
Peter Fisher	49	2	2	3	5
Henry Fager	200	2	3	1	12
Paul Fager	--	1	--	--	1
Idle Gearhart	100	2	2	4	4
Jonas Griffith	--	1	1	--	1
Jas. Gahagan	--	1	--	--	1
John Griner	160	4	6	12	16
Mary Gibson	30	--	--	--	1
Mathias Herner	100	3	2	3	6
Henry Harner	34	--	2	--	2
Fred'k Herner	110	2	3	--	5
John Huling	150	3	5	6	14
Mounce Jones	195	4	4	10	14
Jonas Jones	200	3	6	12	8
Nicho's Jones	50	2	3	9	6
Peter Jones	200	4	2	6	16
Fran's Knows	--	1	1	--	1
John Lorah	200	4	4	6	25
Eleanor Lutz, Wid.	160	4	5	8	16
For E. Griffith, dec'd	112	--	--	--	8
Michael Lop	--	--	--	--	1
Henry Lear	100	1	2	4	5
John Moudy	150	--	1	--	8
Martin Marquart	167	2	3	5	5
John Moyer	400	4	4	--	20
Henry Miller	100	2	2	--	6
Geo. Marsteller	--	1	--	--	1
John Old	150	--	--	--	14
Henry Pot	50	1	2	--	4
Thomas Paine, inn keeper	--	1	1	--	2
Jacob Rhoads, p.m.	185	5	6	10	26
Len'd Rodarmal, b'smith	--	1	2	2	2
Ludwig Rodarmal	--	--	1	--	1
John Sands, g. & s.m.	200	4	6	12	20
Sam'l Sands	--	1	1	6	2
Abijah Sands	160	4	8	7	12
Michael Trump	67	2	3	--	6
Henry Vanreed	150	4	4	10	20
Eliz'a Womelsdorf, g. & p.m.	200	4	6	7	26
David Wadner	--	--	1	5	1
Jacob Waren	17	2	2	--	3
Thomas Waren	100	3	2	6	8
William Winter	470	4	6	10	28
Jos. Webb	200	4	2	--	8
Wm. Williams	--	1	1	--	1

Amity Township	Acres	Horses	Cattle	Sheep	Tax
Jacob Weaver	12	2	2	--	5
Peter Weaver	400	3	4	8	20
Joseph Williams	--	1	1	--	1
Benj'a Williams	120	2	2	7	2
John Teeter	202	2	--	--	5
John Sands, Jr.	100	--	--	--	5

Single Men

	Shillings		Shillings
John Crane	15	And'w Ralphsnider	15
John Lincker	15	Chas. Bell	15
Mat's Rhoads	15	Da'd Williams	15
Jacob Rhoads	15	Jeremiah Bryan	15
Jas. McGowen	15	Mich'l Bower	15
Joseph Sands	15	Leonard Holman	15
Peter Isaminger	15	John Dieter	15
Hen. Gamwell	15	Jacob Fager	15
Geo. Womelsdorf	15	Jno. Swartboug	15
Abijah Sands	15	Sam'l Dehart	15
Jonas Jones	15	Michael Miller	15
Nicho's Jones	15	John Sands	15
Tobias Kelley	15	Geo. Lutz	15
Abram Enoch	15	Peter Croop	15
Martin Overmiller	15	Philip Croop	15
Boltzer Gear	15	Casper Croop	15
Wm. Janet	15	Jacob Struble	15
Jno. Ralphsnider	15	Mich'l Everhart	15

Maiden Creek Township

	Acres	Horses	Cattle	Sheep	Tax
John Aurandt, farmer	200	3	3	3	12
William Adams, carpenter	--	--	--	--	1
Stephen Bernet, farmer	300	4	8	5	20
Wendel Breeder, farmer	100	2	2	2	5
Fred'k Blatt, farmer	100	2	3	3	6
Mathias Braun, weaver	--	--	--	--	1
Simeon Barger, weaver	25	--	1	--	2
Michael Christ, smith & farmer	160	2	2	--	12
Isaac Clendenon, taylor	--	--	--	--	1
Barn'd Curry, labourer	20	1	1	--	2
Dennis Carrol, labourer	50	--	1	1	2
Michael Dunkle, labourer	150	4	6	6	15
Jacob Eckell, farmer	150	4	4	--	12
Adam Engel, farmer	50	2	2	--	3
George Fegelle, farmer	200	3	4	4	10
John Frauenfelder, farmer	150	2	3	8	8
George Gernant, farmer	300	4	4	4	20
Jacob Greff, farmer	200	5	4	3	12
John Gumber, farmer	70	2	3	3	4
Owen Hughes, farmer	500	4	7	10	30

49

Maiden Creek Township	Acres	Horses	Cattle	Sheep	Tax
James Hutton, farmer, s.m.	460	4	7	10	28
John Hutten, farmer	200	3	4	6	20
Jacob High, farmer	170	2	3	4	12
Rudolph High, farmer	168	4	4	5	14
Valentine Hofman, shoemaker	--	1	2	--	2
Wm. Houlden, mason	--	--	1	--	1
Jacob Hofhans, Sen., farmer	600	--	--	1	30
Casper Jost, farmer	100	1	1	--	6
Timothy Jennings, labourer	--	--	1	--	1
Ulrick Hug, farmer	350	5	4	10	20
John Kaufman, farmer	178	3	6	6	15
John Koch, farmer	250	4	4	5	23
Thomas Kutz, taverner	70	2	2	--	6
Standley Kerby, farmer	300	6	12	8	25
Abraham Kiesinger, carpenter	--	--	--	--	1
Martin Kirschman, carpenter	--	1	2	--	2
Valentine Keim, farmer	180	4	5	6	12
John Kranshar, laborer	--	--	1	--	1
John Klein, farmer	50	2	2	--	3
Mordecai Lee, farmer	350	4	10	6	28
Anthony Lee, farmer, s.m.	240	3	3	5	25
Jacob Lightfoot, farmer	200	6	7	26	10
Jacob Lupfer	50	--	--	--	4
David Miller, labourer	--	--	1	1	2
Jacob Maurer, farmer	150	4	6	8	10
Francis Parvin, landholder, s. & g.m.	900	2	2	7	40
Joseph Penrose, farmer	280	4	5	10	20
Fran's Parvin, Jr., farmer	--	1	3	11	2
Wm. Parvin, miller	--	1	2	2	1
Thomas Parvin, farmer	--	2	2	--	3
Thomas Pearson, weaver	--	--	1	1	2
John Starr	210	7	8	10	18
Merick Starr, farmer	150	3	4	10	10
Moses Starr, Jr., farmer	135	2	3	4	8
John Schneider, weaver	110	1	2	--	7
Jacob Scheffer, farmer	149	2	2	--	12
Frantz Shalter, farmer	130	2	2	--	8
John Reeser, farmer	400	4	6	8	24
Paul Rothermal, farmer	260	4	6	11	15
Peter Rothermal, farmer	200	5	4	6	12
Christian Richstein, farmer	150	2	4	--	9
Jacob Rann	150	--	--	--	8
Elias Reed, farmer	100	3	5	--	5
Christopher Ring, labourer	--	--	--	--	1
Geo. Reseler, farmer	100	2	2	--	5
Michael Tompson	--	--	--	--	1
Jacob Zech, farmer	100	2	3	2	6
Thos. Winckler, farmer	50	2	2	3	3
Joseph Weily, weaver	--	--	--	--	2
Henry Frey, farmer	150	3	2	--	15
Martin Houseman, farmer	150	4	2	--	10

Single Men

	Shillings		Shillings
Isaac Barger	15	Peter Rothermal	15
John Richardson	15	Mich'l Kirby	15
Thos. McGlasky	15	Peter Clementz	15
John Parvin	15	Henry Hartman	15
John Barger	15	Adam Texter	15
Thos. Lightfoot	15	Abram Huy	15
Edw'd Kinsler	15	George Reem	15
Thomas Cross	15		

Robeson Township

	Acres	Horses	Cattle	Sheep	Tax
George Adam, b'smith	--	--	1	--	1
Daniel Bosserd, farmer	100	2	2	--	4
Daniel Beean	200	2	3	3	9
Nicholas Beiss	100	2	2	--	4
Michael Beard	75	2	2	--	3
Peter Beam, b'smith	100	2	2	--	4
Conrad Beitler, s.m.	200	3	4	2	16
John Bayer, g.m.	100	2	2	3	7
Thomas Berry	--	1	2	3	3
Walter Burck	--	2	2	--	2
Christian Bixler	200	2	3	2	10
Peter Bauman	100	2	4	2	10
John Cadwalader	50	--	1	--	1
Gaius Dickinson	300	2	3	10	12
Geo. Dunahaur	50	1	2	1	2
Joseph Davis	25	2	2	--	1
Stephen Doughten	--	2	4	10	2
Pennal Evans	120	2	3	--	20
Christian Ergot	150	2	4	5	6
Daniel Evans	100	2	2	2	3
Valentine Emms	200	3	3	3	15
John Evans	--	--	2	--	1
Stephen Francis	--	2	2	--	2
Edward Goff	100	2	2	6	6
Christoph'r Geiger	200	4	5	6	20
Ellis George, weaver	100	2	2	6	3
John Griffith	50	2	2	--	2
God. John Guldin	--	1	1	--	1
Richard George	100	2	4	7	8
Edward George	80	2	2	3	2
John Garrett	--	1	2	--	1
Paul Geiger	150	3	4	6	11
William Iddings	170	3	6	6	7
Valentine Hahn	150	3	5	6	15
Philip Hartz	35	1	2	--	2
Peter Hecker	--	1	1	--	1
Philip Hail	100	2	1	2	4
Michael Hermer, weaver	100	--	1	--	2
Owen Humphrey, s.m.	100	2	4	5	10
Valentine Kerbery, shoemaker	50	1	1	--	2

51

Robeson Township	Acres	Horses	Cattle	Sheep	Tax
Ephraim Jackson, Jr.	--	1	5	6	3
Ephraim Jackson, Sen'r	140	2	4	6	10
David Jackson	--	1	1	3	2
James James	--	1	1	--	1
George Jock	--	1	1	--	1
Jacob Lang	--	--	--	--	--
Owen Long	100	2	2	4	3
Sam'l Overholtzer	50	2	1	--	2
Nicho's Miller	--	2	3	4	2
Conrad Moore	200	3	3	6	6
David Marris	100	--	2	1	3
Richard Nusam, b'smith	100	2	1	--	5
Henry Pennebecker	247	3	5	6	16
John Philip	150	2	3	--	3
John Phrees	100	2	3	4	6
Paul Reily	100	2	2	4	4
Henry Richard	100	2	--	--	3
Israel Robinson	400	2	2	3	22
Elias Ratge	140	4	4	6	11
John Ringler	100	2	2	--	3
Thomas Robinson	100	1	1	4	2
Andreas Moore	100	2	1	--	3
Arnold Sheffer	100	2	2	--	5
Peter Sell	50	2	2	3	2
Adam Steal	--	3	4	4	3
Michael Snoufer	80	2	2	4	4
Herman Snider	100	2	2	2	4
John Shields	--	--	1	--	1
John Scarlet	400	4	8	14	14
Jonathan Stephen, weaver	180	2	2	--	5
Melchior Swizer	100	2	2	3	4
Thomas Thomas	300	3	5	6	15
David Thomas, millwright	260	2	2	5	9
James Thomas	150	2	4	4	4
Harman Umsted	200	4	7	5	13
Jonathan Worrel	100	2	2	--	5
Geo. Wolf	100	2	2	2	5
Geo. Wentel	200	2	2	--	5
Paul Wall	40	1	1	--	2
Baltzer King	100	1	1	--	2
Mark Licken	50	1	1	--	2
Caleb Jones	140	2	2	6	6
W'm Humphrey	60	--	--	--	2
Benjamin Wells	80	2	2	--	8
Richard Auty	--	2	2	7	1
John Goheen	60	--	--	--	2
W'm Douglas	50	--	--	--	2
Jno. Jenkin	95	--	--	--	3
Henry Gable	40	1	1	--	2
Adam Layer	--	--	1	--	1
David Stephens	400	--	--	--	20
Peter Angstat	50	--	--	--	7
Jacob Wert	100	2	3	6	4
Michael Hofman	100	--	--	--	2
Sam'l Griffith	50	--	--	--	2

Robeson Township	Acres	Horses	Cattle	Sheep	Tax
John Meyer	150	--	--	--	4
George Sower	40	--	1	--	2
Thomas May	150	--	--	--	5
Mich'l Thornton	--	--	1	--	1
Geo. Taylor	150	--	--	--	6
Rob't Levers	200	--	--	--	6
Sam'l Keys	--	2	1	--	1
Ad. Barner	--	--	1	--	1
W'm Key	--	1	1	--	1
Capt'n Flower, & Co.	500	--	--	--	25
Rev'd Alex'r Murray	155	--	--	--	3

Single Men

	Shillings		Shillings
Peter Licken	15	Geo. Snouffer	15
Casper Wolf	15	Jas. Treeby	15
Paul Person	15	Jacob Snouffer	15
John Sprogel	15	W'm Scarlet	15
Bernhard Eargot	15	Daniel Trumpp	15
Jacob Eargot	15	Henry Wagoner	15
Elias Ratge	15	Tho's Davis	15
Tho's Treeby	15		

Tulpehoccon Township

	Acres	Horses	Cattle	Sheep	Tax
Leonard Anspach	200	2	2	2	13
Geo. Anspach	5	--	--	--	1
Jacob Artz	100	2	2	2	4
Jacob Anspach	100	2	2	--	3
Peter Aman	50	1	2	--	2
Hans Alwerd, g.m.	100	2	3	3	8
Adam Alwerd	50	1	1	--	2
Michael Alwerd	40	2	3	--	4
Hans Ahe	50	2	2	--	3
Peter Anspach	150	3	2	--	18
Hans Anspach	150	3	2	1	18
Dan'l Aulenbach	100	2	1	--	4
Bastian Brosius	200	2	2	2	6
Philip Brua	100	4	2	2	12
Christ'n Brichdel, potter	75	2	4	6	5
Cha's Bomberger, tanner	75	.2	2	2	5
Jacob Beek	50	1	1	--	1
Herber Berger	50	2	1	--	2
Max Breying	50	1	1	--	2
Bernhard Beck	50	1	1	--	2
John Braun	60	4	2	--	10
Martin Braun	50	2	2	--	8
Geo. Boltz	100	2	2	--	4
Jacob Bretzius	30	1	1	--	3
Adam Braddecker	60	1	2	--	3
Simon Brosius	100	5	3	--	5

Tulpehoccon Township	Acres	Horses	Cattle	Sheep	Tax
Michael Decker, g.m.	150	4	3	4	6
Geo. Dollinger	150	3	4	7	7
Nicholas Deck	30	1	2	--	2
Frederick Deck	77	1	2	--	2
Fredrick Degler, smith	50	2	2	4	2
Rudolph Dedweiler	90	2	2	4	4
Jost Derr	50	2	2	4	4
Adam Defenbach	100	2	4	2	15
Eva Draudmenen	100	2	2	2	5
Jacob Dondore	200	--	2	2	10
Andreas Eders	100	3	2	2	7
Jacob Echsberger	150	3	4	5	14
Baltzer Emrich	50	1	2	--	3
Adam Emrich	112	2	2	2	14
John Eckerd	50	2	2	2	6
Christian Frantz	200	2	2	4	10
Ulrich Fisher	100	2	2	2	3
Nicholas Frenger	50	2	2	--	2
Michael Forri	119	3	4	3	13
Geo. Faust	50	2	4	--	2
Geo. Fengle	60	2	1	--	2
Jacob Fisher	145	4	3	3	16
Hanes Gerwirich	100	3	2	3	2
Jacob Geper	100	2	3	3	4
Philip Gebhard	100	2	3	--	9
Nicholas Gaucker	100	2	2	2	3
Geo. Grist	90	--	1	--	2
Jacob Gicker	25	2	2	--	2
Henry Gadman	40	1	1	--	3
Cather Gissemenen	50	--	2	--	2
Christian Gruber	100	2	3	2	7
John Gwist	40	1	1	--	1
Hanes Gebhard	50	1	2	--	9
Henry Groff, smith	100	3	3	--	8
Hanes Hahn	80	3	2	2	3
Mich'l Hamburger	50	2	2	--	2
Hanes Holff, cooper	20	--	1	--	2
Hanes Hubler	100	2	3	--	5
Hans Heverling	50	1	1	1	3
Geo. Haug	40	3	3	2	2
Nicho's Haug	100	3	3	2	5
Casper Hinkle	70	2	4	4	6
Peter Heckman	237	4	6	5	10
Fred'k Holtzman	100	3	2	2	5
Albert Hey	150	5	4	6	5
Charles Hey	100	2	2	3	6
John Hes	100	2	2	--	4
Adam Jacobi	50	1	1	--	2
Henry Keblinger, smith	50	2	2	--	4
Jacob Katterman	150	3	3	2	10
Thomas Kurr	300	4	4	8	12
Peter Krieger	150	2	2	--	7
Fred'k Keiser	100	2	3	2	13
Hans Kofman	30	2	1	--	2
Michael Keyser	50	1	1	--	3

Tulpehoccon Township	Acres	Horses	Cattle	Sheep	Tax
Peter Kreitzer	50	2	2	2	4
Jacob Kandner	150	2	2	3	6
Simon Kroh	50	2	1	--	2
Christian Kerner	100	2	2	--	5
Michael Kedner	150	3	2	2	7
Philip Klar	30	--	1	--	2
Mathias Kembf	50	1	1	--	3
Stophel Kern	100	2	2	--	3
Simon Kern	30	1	1	--	2
William Keiser	100	2	2	2	6
Nicho's Kintzer, smith	150	4	4	7	19
Michael Kortz	40	2	2	--	4
Hanes Kortz	100	4	4	4	16
George Kantner	100	4	4	4	9
George Klein	50	2	2	4	5
Geo. Ludwig	100	2	2	--	4
Jacob Levengud	300	4	4	6	30
Hans Lescher	30	2	2	--	3
Geo. Lechner, g.m. & s.m.	150	5	3	--	35
Peter Lebo, Jun'r	30	2	3	--	2
Peter Lebo, Sen'r	80	2	2	--	4
Hans Lingle	100	2	1	--	3
Nicholas Lang	100	2	2	2	7
W'm Leidner	100	2	2	--	3
Casper Lang	40	1	1	--	1
Jacob Loss	60	2	2	--	5
Geo. Lauckes	50	3	2	--	6
Peter Leys	100	3	3	2	12
Peter Letterman	100	4	2	8	7
Christian Lauer, g.m., s.m.	450	7	6	--	55
Abram Lauck	100	3	2	2	19
Dewald Laucks	30	1	1	1	2
Henry Meyer	250	4	3	8	12
Geo. Meyer	100	1	2	1	6
Christian Meyer	75	1	2	--	3
Nicholas Miller	50	2	2	--	3
Hanes Meyer	50	2	1	--	3
Jacob Milleisen	50	2	2	--	3
Philip Meyer	30	2	2	--	3
Jacob Miller	50	2	2	--	2
Philip Meyer	100	3	3	4	13
Hans Merky	1	--	1	--	3
Mat's Miller	100	2	2	2	8
Hanes Miller	100	2	2	2	8
Valentine Meyer	150	4	4	10	7
Mich'l Nashack	50	1	1	--	2
Baltzer Nol	100	2	2	2	7
Valentine Ney	150	1	2	2	5
Mat's Nafzger	140	3	4	6	10
Peter Prua	100	3	2	--	8
Jacob Peyffer	50	2	1	--	2
Hans Puntzius	50	2	2	1	5
Hans Paffenberger	40	3	3	3	5
Mich'l Paffenberger	50	4	1	2	9
Casper Reed	100	3	2	2	6

Tulpehoccon Township	Acres	Horses	Cattle	Sheep	Tax
Jacob Reed	100	2	3	--	7
Dan'l Reed	100	3	2	2	13
Casper Reed	100	3	3	2	18
Godfred Rohrer	150	3	3	2	8
Geo. Reed, j'r., g.m.	50	2	2	--	4
Peter Ritzman	50	2	2	--	3
Hans Reidenour	100	2	2	--	3
Conrad Rever	100	2	2	3	4
Adam Rim	50	2	2	--	2
Hanes Rohn	100	2	2	2	2
Dan'l Riegel	50	2	2	--	6
Simon Riegel	100	3	2	2	9
Casper Reed, j'r.	150	4	3	3	16
Hans Reys	150	4	2	6	30
Nicho's Reed	170	3	4	4	20
Leonard Rid	80	3	3	4	150
Peter Reed	100	3	2	--	10
Fred'k Reid	180	3	3	--	17
Michael Reed	130	4	4	4	14
Geo. Reed	140	4	2	2	18
Valentine Rentzel	100	2	2	2	6
Geo. Radenbach	50	2	2	--	5
Jost Reidel	70	2	2	4	6
Hans Riegel, g.m.	150	4	3	4	20
Hans Schitz	100	4	3	3	20
Christian Seiwerd	70	2	3	2	4
Nicholas Seiwerd	80	3	--	3	6
Hans Schneh	100	2	1	--	2
Mich'l Schwartz	150	3	3	3	6
Henry Scheffer, wag'ner	100	2	2	--	3
Stophel Schum, taylor	30	1	1	--	2
George Stauch, wag'ner	100	2	2	--	3
Mich'l Sausser, joiner	15	1	2	1	2
And's Saltzgeber, sadler	10	--	1	--	21
Abram Schneider	100	2	2	2	4
Nich's Schlesman	100	3	1	--	5
Nicholas Scheffer	100	2	2	2	6
Peter Speyger	70	2	2	--	2
Henry Schebler, g.m., s.m.	40	2	2	--	5
Andreas Schod	60	2	2	2	3
Adam Scheffer	50	3	4	4	5
Hanes Schob	50	2	2	2	4
Adam Strum	50	2	2	2	6
Geo. Shirman	100	2	2	2	5
Hen. Stiegle, & Co., s.m.	80	12	--	--	45
Hans Scheffer, j'r.	150	4	4	6	25
Hans Scheffer	100	2	2	--	8
Peter Scheffer	100	4	4	5	18
Peter Spicker, Esq'r	66	3	1	--	25
Benja. Spicker	40	1	2	--	10
Adam Schmid	100	2	2	--	5
Jacob Schmid	100	2	2	--	4
Casper Stumb	100	3	3	4	18
Maria Sollenbergerin	90	2	2	3	6
Adam Schirman	200	3	3	3	9

Tulpehoccon Township

	Acres	Horses	Cattle	Sheep	Tax
Jacob Scheffer	100	2	2	2	5
George Ulrich	50	--	1	--	2
Valentine Unru	200	2	3	2	30
Hans Wallever	100	2	2	--	3
Hantz Geo. Wolf	100	2	2	4	4
Adam Walborn	100	1	1	--	4
Frederick Winder	50	2	2	3	10
Nicholas Weyand	40	2	3	2	5
Jacob Weiser	200	3	2	2	10
Geo. Walborn	100	1	2	--	6
Geo. Weckler	100	2	2	--	5
Mesger Wolf	100	2	4	--	10
Fred'k Wolf	150	4	3	6	6
Geo. Weber	100	2	2	3	6
Conrad Werd	50	1	2	--	2
W'm Weaber	100	2	3	--	5
Stophel Winder	150	2	3	2	6
Hans Wertz	80	1	2	--	3
Hans Wecksler	100	2	2	--	6
Jacob Wilhelm	100	3	2	--	6
Jacob Wagner	100	2	2	2	6
Hans Zoller	100	4	6	6	16
Geo. Zoller	150	5	4	5	18
Peter Zerwe	100	3	2	4	7
Hans Zerwe	150	2	2	2	9
Philip Ziegler	115	3	4	3	5
Peter Zerven	100	3	3	4	16
Benja. Zerben	20	--	2	2	1
Adam Krickbaum	50	--	--	--	3

	Labourers				Pounds
Wendal Waltz	--	--	--	--	1
Andreas Wolf	--	--	--	--	1
Geo. Sheffer	--	--	--	--	1
Valentine Shuler	--	--	--	--	1
Geo. Schleic	--	--	--	--	1
Conrad Reidenaur	--	--	--	--	1
Geo. Adam	--	--	--	--	1
Hans Miller	--	--	--	--	1
Daniel Lucas	--	--	--	--	1
David Katterman	--	--	--	--	1
Philip Wolfard	--	--	--	--	1
Hanes Keyser	--	--	--	--	1
Hanes Kuhn	--	--	--	--	1
Henry Lebo	--	--	--	--	1
Fred'k Schnack	--	--	--	--	1
Hanes Sugar	--	--	--	--	1
W'm Steyn	--	--	--	--	1
Stoffel Wolfard	--	--	--	--	1
Andreas Kraff	--	--	--	--	1
Christian Wertz	--	--	--	--	1
Ludwig Long	--	--	--	--	1
Frantz Hubler	--	--	--	--	1

Labourers

				Pounds
Henry Radenbach	--	--	--	--	1
Stoffel Stealer	--	--	--	--	1
Nicho's Kuntz	--	--	--	--	1
Conrad Redman	--	--	--	--	1
Mich'l Bretzius	--	--	--	--	1
Conrad Munch	--	--	--	--	1
Hanes Buehler	--	--	--	--	1
Simon Bressler	--	--	--	--	1
George Bressler	--	--	--	--	1
Jacob Lebo	--	--	--	--	1
Sam'l Beyer	--	--	--	--	1
Philip Kleyn	--	--	--	--	1
Nicho's Dormayer	--	--	--	--	1
Jacob Blanck	--	--	--	--	1
Eberhard Geysweid	--	--	--	--	1
Adam Kalbach	--	--	--	--	1
Hans Herr	--	--	--	--	1
Henry Schmid	--	--	--	--	1
Simon Sheffer	--	--	--	--	2
Geo. Scheyle	--	--	--	--	1
Godfrey Kercher	--	--	--	--	1
John Humel	--	--	--	--	1
Mathias Shoch	--	--	--	--	1
Peter Kister	--	--	--	--	1
Nicholas Kilmer	--	--	--	--	2
Jacob Diefenbach	--	--	--	--	1
	--	--	--	--	1

Single Men

Name	Shillings	Name	Shillings
Jacob Heckman	15	Casper Stumpf	15
Geo. Anspach	15	Wendel Graff	15
Peter Laudershcleager	15	Jos. Krebs	15
Mich'l Walborn	15	Jacob Reed	15
Jacob Kondner Jr.	15	Henry Schuck	15
Geo. Kantner	15	Jacob Anspach	15
Simon Geisler	15	Adam Fisher	15
Henry Koch	15	Leonhard Reed	15
Peter Zerve	15	Hans Forrer	15
Hans Faust	15	Philip Reed	15

Bern Township

	Acres	Horses	Cattle	Sheep	Tax
Christian Albrecht, farmer	100	2	3	--	6
Hans Adam, farmer	30	2	2	--	2
Christian Althouse, farmer	100	2	2	2	3
Hans Arbengast, farmer	30	2	2	--	2
Jacob Allwine, shoemaker	100	2	2	4	7
Michael Beier, farmer	80	2	2	--	3
Christian Bens, farmer	--	--	--	--	1
Jacob Bich, farmer	50	2	3	3	2

Bern Township	Acres	Horses	Cattle	Sheep	Tax
Philip Beier, farmer	100	2	3	3	6
Geo. Belleman, farmer	60	2	2	--	4
David Brecht, farmer	150	4	3	3	15
Hans Bucks, farmer	150	2	2	1	12
Jacob Beiler, farmer	178	2	5	4	10
Johannes Berkey, farmer	100	2	4	--	5
Ulrich Backenstos, farmer	100	2	2	3	6
Adam Blatt, farmer	20	--	1	--	2
Adam Bohn, farmer	100	3	3	--	7
Christ'n Berriger, farmer	100	2	3	--	5
Geo. Bender, farmer	50	1	1	2	2
Jacob Beiller, farmer	--	--	--	--	1
Henry Beier, farmer	100	3	3	2	8
Jacob Conrad, farmer	100	3	3	2	9
Jacob Dester, farmer	25	--	--	--	2
Leonard Detrick, farmer	200	2	2	--	12
Mat's Dornbach	150	2	2	--	10
Jacob Ebler, farmer	150	4	5	4	15
Valentine Ebler, farmer	150	2	4	2	12
Geo. Ernst, farmer	100	2	2	--	5
Bastian Emrich, farmer	50	1	1	--	3
Peter Ebler, farmer	150	2	3	4	8
Hannes Faust, farmer	100	2	2	1	5
Philip Faust, farmer	150	2	2	4	8
Henry Fisher	100	2	2	2	6
Samuel Filbert, farmer	100	--	4	2	4
Philip Fucks, farmer	150	2	2	--	9
Henry Freyman	50	1	1	--	3
Frederick Frum, farmer	100	2	2	--	6
Adam German, farmer	50	2	2	--	3
Michael Graul, farmer	50	--	2	2	--
Jacob Gisline, farmer	50	--	2	2	2
Henry Gicker, farmer	80	2	2	3	4
Jacob Gintelberger, farmer	100	--	1	2	6
Eberhard Gesweidt, farmer	100	2	3	4	6
Jacob Grim, farmer	50	--	1	1	3
David Grim, farmer	100	2	2	--	5
Jacob Grim, shoemaker	100	2	2	--	6
Geo. Grusel, farmer	50	1	1	--	4
Philip Jacob Geis, farmer	50	2	2	--	3
Geo. Adam Geis, farmer	30	2	2	--	2
Christ'r Godtshal, farmer	50	2	1	--	3
Jacob Hochstetler, farmer	60	1	1	--	4
Jost Heister, farmer	100	2	3	1	6
Peter Harpine, farmer	100	2	2	3	7
Jacob Hertzler, farmer	150	2	3	4	9
Geo. Hauber, farmer	--	--	--	--	1
Conrad Heany, farmer	100	1	1	--	7
Hans Hockstetler, farmer	80	2	2	--	5
Peter Herschberger, farmer	--	--	--	--	--
George Hainer, farmer	30	1	1	--	3
Philip Hein, farmer	--	--	--	--	--
Wm. Hettrich, farmer	100	2	2	--	8
Hieronimus Henig, taverner	50	2	4	--	4
John Nich's Hollar, farmer	150	3	3	4	10

Bern Township	Acres	Horses	Cattle	Sheep	Tax
John Heck, farmer	150	3	3	4	12
Abram Haas, farmer	50	2	2	--	3
Christ'n Hershberger, farmer	50	2	2	3	4
Felty Himelberger, farmer	100	2	2	3	5
Jacob Heck, farmer	100	2	2	--	5
Daniel Heister, farmer	150	--	--	--	14
Christian Joder, farmer	100	2	3	4	7
Hanes Joder	150	--	--	--	9
Christian Joder, farmer	100	2	3	2	8
Henry Klos, farmer	20	1	1	--	3
Stephen Kaufman, farmer	100	2	2	3	5
Mich'l Kisinger, farmer	100	2	2	--	5
John Klauser, farmer	100	2	2	3	5
Jacob Kaufman, farmer	100	2	--	3	6
Isaac Kaufman, farmer	100	--	--	--	5
Mich'l Kuntfer, farmer	100	4	3	--	5
Benedict Kepler, farmer, g.m.	100	2	4	8	6
Margt. Kaufman, wid'o	60	2	2	--	3
Stephen Kurtz, farmer	100	2	3	3	6
Henry Ketner, farmer	60	2	2	3	4
Michael Kiel, farmer	150	3	3	4	9
Conrad Kerschner, farmer	--	--	--	--	--
Martin Kerschner, farmer	100	2	4	4	7
John Klein, farmer	100	2	2	--	4
Margt. Klein, Wid'o	100	2	2	--	4
Stephen Kreider, farmer	--	--	--	--	--
Bernhard Kepener, farmer	100	1	1	--	4
Geo. Ludwig, farmer	60	2	2	--	3
Sam'l Lightfoot, gent.	500	--	--	--	30
John Long, farmer	150	2	2	--	9
John Felty Long, farmer	100	2	3	4	6
Baltzer Lerrich, farmer	--	--	--	--	1
Fredrich Long, farmer	100	2	2	--	5
Mich'l Lindemuth, farmer	100	2	3	--	4
Benedic Lehman, farmer	100	2	3	2	6
Jacob Link, farmer	50	1	1	--	2
Geo. Loos, farmer	100	2	1	--	4
Hans Wm. Leimister, farmer	200	2	2	--	10
Peter Lehr, farmer	--	--	--	--	1
Christian Lick, farmer	--	--	--	--	1
Wm. Lerck, farmer	100	4	2	--	5
Jno. Jacob Long, farmer	--	--	--	--	1
Michael Lerrick, farmer	--	--	--	--	1
Michael Moser, farmer	100	2	2	3	5
Geo. Mettler, farmer	60	1	1	--	3
Philip Machamer, farmer	100	2	2	--	4
Hans Marshall, farmer	50	2	2	--	3
Lenhardt Minich, farmer	--	--	--	--	1
Sam'l Miller, farmer	40	1	1	--	2
Felty Mogle, farmer	60	1	1	--	3
Michael Miller, farmer	20	1	1	--	2
Adam Mattern, farmer	30	1	1	3	2
Lucas Moyer, farmer	--	--	--	--	1
Weyerly Moser, farmer	150	2	2	2	8
Jacob Miller, farmer	100	3	3	2	5

Bern Township	Acres	Horses	Cattle	Sheep	Tax
John Meyer, farmer	50	1	1	--	2
Jacob Mast, farmer	100	2	2	--	4
Jacob Minich, farmer	100	2	2	--	4
Geo. Mich'l Minich, farmer	100	2	2	--	4
Christ'n Minich, farmer	80	2	1	--	3
Nicholas Miller, farmer	100	2	2	--	7
Geo. Moyer, farmer	40	1	1	--	2
Martin Noecker, farmer	150	2	4	3	8
Ludwig Nichola, farmer	50	2	--	--	3
Mat's Naftzher, farmer	100	2	2	3	4
Godfred Orbig, farmer	--	--	--	--	1
Joseph Obald, farmer	100	2	2	3	4
Nicho's Meier, farmer	50	1	1	--	3
Benj'a Parvin, surveyor	50	--	--	--	2
Thos. Parvin, farmer	--	--	--	--	2
Casper Philip, farmer	80	1	1	--	3
Ludwig Peiffer, farmer	--	--	--	--	1
Benjamin Right, farmer	50	1	2	6	3
Philip Reiser, farmer	150	3	8	6	20
Henry Reiser, farmer	150	3	6	4	20
Conrad Reel, farmer	--	--	--	--	1
Mich'l Renschler, farmer	50	2	2	4	3
Hans Raver, farmer	100	2	2	--	10
Ulrich Radmacher, taylor	100	2	2	--	6
Hans Runkel, farmer	100	2	2	--	4
Bastian Ruth, farmer	100	2	3	--	9
Jacob Reicher, farmer	100	2	2	--	7
Herman Rick, farmer	100	2	2	--	7
Peter Radabach, farmer	50	2	1	--	2
Nicho's Runkel, farmer	100	2	1	--	4
Jacob Roodt, farmer	100	--	2	2	5
Geo. Riehm, farmer	100	2	2	--	6
Christian Ruth, farmer	200	4	4	--	10
Michael Reit, farmer	50	1	1	--	3
Jost Shumaker, farmer	50	2	2	3	3
Philip Straus, farmer	100	2	2	2	4
Jacob Straus, farmer	50	2	1	--	2
Michael Spycker, farmer	60	2	2	--	4
Henry Staley, farmer	--	--	--	--	1
Konrad Schnider, farmer	50	2	2	--	3
Max Swinck, farmer	--	--	--	--	--
Mich'l Suber, farmer	--	--	--	--	1
Ludwig Seaman, farmer	100	2	4	2	3
Hans Swartzhaub, farmer	--	--	--	--	1
Thos. Tomlinson, farmer	50	1	1	3	2
Wm. Tomlinson, farmer	150	2	6	12	9
Jost Toby, farmer	50	2	2	--	4
Baltzer Umbehacker, farmer	150	2	2	3	8
Joseph Wolenson, farmer	50	2	2	1	3
John Weidenhamer, farmer	100	2	2	4	6
Sam'l Wolinson, farmer	100	2	4	2	7
Christ'r Wagoner, farmer	100	2	2	--	6
Jacob Wagner, farmer	80	2	2	--	4
Wm. Weaver, farmer	80	2	2	6	5
Philip Wagner, farmer	100	2	2	6	6

Bern Township	Acres	Horses	Cattle	Sheep	Tax
Geo. Ad. Wagner, farmer	100	2	2	--	5
Geo. Wagner, farmer	100	2	2	--	6
Nicho's Weininger, farmer	100	2	1	--	5
Conrad Winckler, farmer	--	--	--	--	--
Johan Worheim, farmer	--	1	2	--	1
Andreas Winter, farmer	150	1	2	--	8
Mich'l Womer, farmer	100	2	2	--	5
Mich'l Womer, farmer	150	2	2	--	8
Jacob Walter, farmer	25	--	1	--	3
Mich'l Winghardt, farmer	--	--	--	--	1
Herman Weaver, farmer	100	2	3	2	7
Hen. Weaver, farmer	--	--	--	--	1
Math's Weaver, farmer	100	4	4	6	8
David Windermuth, farmer	40	1	2	--	3
Peter Zerbe, farmer	100	2	3	3	10
Moritz Zug, farmer	100	3	3	4	15
Mich'l Zuber, farmer	50	1	1	--	3
Jacob Shomaker, farmer	30	--	--	--	3
John Seiber, farmer	250	4	4	2	18
Albrecht Strauss, farmer	100	3	3	4	6
Mich'l Stradt, farmer	100	2	3	--	7
Hans Souder, farmer	100	2	2	--	6
Paul Scheffer, farmer	--	--	--	--	1
John Seitz, farmer	--	--	--	--	--
John Schock, farmer	60	2	2	2	3
Daniel Schlaubach, farmer	50	2	3	--	3
Yost Schlaubach, farmer	100	2	3	2	6
Carl Smith, farmer	100	2	2	2	7
Hans Schnider, farmer	100	2	2	4	8
Jacob Stein, farmer	100	2	1	--	4
Kasper Stein, farmer	--	--	--	--	4
Hans Sneider, Jr., farmer	100	2	2	--	6
Joseph Sumbro, farmer	80	2	2	--	4
Philip Seifert, farmer	30	2	1	--	3
Jost Shoemaker, farmer	--	--	--	--	1
Christ'n Stutzman, farmer	100	2	2	3	10
Geo. Seehman, farmer	--	--	--	--	--
Jacob Schartel, farmer	100	2	2	--	6
Josh. Sollenberger, farmer	50	1	1	--	3
Peter Schamo, farmer	--	--	--	--	1
Verner Stam, farmer	100	2	2	--	8
Mat's Staut, farmer	100	2	2	--	8
Henry Seidle, farmer	100	2	2	--	9
Joseph Schomo, farmer	10	1	2	--	6
Eberhard Smith, farmer	100	3	3	1	10

Single Men

	Shillings		Shillings
John Staudt	15	Philip Himelberger	15
Martin Moor	15	Philip Heck	15
Abram Clay	15	Johannes Staley	15
Jacob Wagoner	15	Peter Zuber	15
Dan'l Althouse	15		

INDEX

INDEX